Santa Fe Hispanic Culture

La Conquistadora, 1948. Photo by Robert H. Martin. La Conquistadora as she appeared in the Rosario Chapel during the Santa Fe Fiesta of 1948. Courtesy the Museum of New Mexico, #41984.

SANTA FE
HISPANIC CULTURE

Preserving Identity in

a Tourist Town

Andrew Leo Lovato

UNIVERSITY OF NEW MEXICO PRESS

ALBUQUERQUE

YEAR   PRINTING
10 09 08 07 06   1 2 3 4 5

PAPERBOUND ISBN-13: 978-0-8263-3226-4
PAPERBOUND ISBN-10: 0-8263-3226-9

Library of Congress Cataloging-in-Publication Data

Lovato, Andrew Leo, 1955–
  Santa Fe Hispanic culture : preserving identity in a tourist town /
Andrew Leo Lovato.— 1st ed.
     p. cm.
  Includes bibliographical references and index.
  ISBN 0-8263-3225-0 (cloth : alk. paper)
  1. Hispanic Americans—New Mexico—Santa Fe—Ethnic identity. 2.
Hispanic Americans—New Mexico—Santa Fe—History. 3. Santa Fe
(N.M.)—Civilization. I. Title.
  F804.S29S75 2004
  305.868'073'0978956—dc22

                               2004015735

DESIGN AND COMPOSITION: Mina Yamashita

Dedicated to Dr. Everett M. Rogers,

my teacher, mentor and friend.

I am truly fortunate

to be counted among those you have

inspired over the years.

❧

Table of Contents

LIST OF FIGURES

LIST OF TABLES

Preface

The afternoon of Sunday, September 12, 1999, was a typically sunny day in Santa Fe, New Mexico. As I sat on the curb in front of the Santa Fe Public Library on Washington Avenue, I could not help but smile at the scene that passed before my eyes. I was witnessing the *Desfile de la Fiesta*, more commonly known as the Historical/Hysterical Parade, one of the highlights of the 287th Fiesta de Santa Fe.

To the uninitiated, the scene might have seemed surreal. The parade procession included the 1999 Fiesta Queen (who was my sister); the honorary Don Diego De Vargas and his *Cuadrilla* (staff); local politicians waving to the crowds in souped-up, lowrider cars; an Elvis impersonator; a four-piece band in the back of a pickup truck playing "La Bamba"; body-builders lifting weights on a flatbed truck; high school marching bands; floats advertising local businesses including a funeral home, pizza place, and motorcycle shop; a huge snorting papier-maché bull with flashing eyes promoting the Rodeo de Santa Fe; senior citizens in buses throwing candy to the crowd; and lots of horses.

This colorful collage that paraded through the streets of downtown Santa Fe during the 1999 Fiesta was in some ways a reflection of the nature and character of the Santa Fe that has evolved through the years and that exists today.

Santa Fe is a city of ancient traditions, but also, as Chris Wilson (1997) stated, of "invented traditions." It is deeply influenced by its cultural roots, while at the same time it has been willing to reshape and commodify its cultural symbols for sale to the highest bidder. It is both a small town and rather cosmopolitan in its ambiance. In short, Santa Fe is a tourist town, a community that reveres its roots and simultaneously generates its livelihood from those roots.

As a native Hispanic resident of Santa Fe, I have witnessed these contradictions and experienced this unique blend of fact and fantasy in blatant forms and on tacit levels.

As I began to conduct the initial research for this book, many Santa Feans expressed their support. During Santa Fe's annual Spanish Market in 1999, for example, I spoke to a number of Hispanic artists about my manuscript. A frequently expressed theme was that it is important for local Hispanics to write about their own culture rather than for outside observers to do so. These comments, which mirror sentiments I have heard several times since, provided inspiration to pursue this project.

Edward T. Hall (1959), the founder of the field of intercultural communication and a resident of Santa Fe, stated in his pioneering work *The Silent Language*, "Simply learning one's own culture is an achievement of gargantuan proportions" (p. 30). Later, he wrote:

> Years of study have convinced me that the real job is not to understand foreign culture but our own. I am also convinced that all one ever gets from studying foreign culture is a token understanding. The ultimate reason for such study is to learn more about how one's own system works. (Hall, 1959, p. 30)

Acknowledgments

Dr. John Condon, Professor Miguel Gandert, and Dr. Enrique Lamadrid, thank you for your input, support, and encouragement.

Special thanks to Dr. Everett M. Rogers, whose guidance and contributions were invaluable in the completion of this book.

CHAPTER ONE

Introduction

Every culture creates its own perceptual

worlds. And until this fact is learned by

the human species, horrendous distortions

in understanding are inevitable.

(Hall, 1986, p. xvii)

The Sangre de Cristo Mountains surround the city of Santa Fe, creating a vista for one of the most celebrated tourist destinations in the world. According to the Santa Fe Convention and Visitors Bureau, in 2003 more than one million visitors from throughout the globe visited New Mexico's state capital to experience "The City Different." The fascination that visitors have for Santa Fe can be attributed in part to the city's natural attractions. Santa Fe averages over three hundred days of sunshine a year, and the high mountain air and surrounding landscape lend themselves to startling blue skies and spectacular sunsets. Many observers comment on the magical quality of the natural light of Santa Fe, an attribute of the city that has drawn many artists. However, there are many locations in New Mexico and beyond that match Santa Fe in natural beauty. The special draw that Santa Fe has on visitors springs not only from its geographical attributes but is due in large part to its image as a "cultural mecca." Lucy Lippard (1999) referred to this phenomenon, in her book *On the Beaten Track*, as "cultural tourism." She divided cultural tourism into three areas: (1) arts tourism, (2) history tourism, and (3) ethnotourism. Lippard's three components reflect Santa Fe's appeal as a tourist destination.

Certainly the arts are a major factor in Santa Fe's popularity. The 2004 Santa Fe Visitors Guide, published by the Santa Fe Convention and Visitor's Bureau proudly points out that *Travel and Leisure* magazine rates Santa Fe as its third most popular travel destination in North America and tenth in the world. *American Style* magazine also consistently names Santa Fe among the top art destinations in the country.

Santa Fe is home to over 250 art businesses employing approximately ten thousand residents, or about one out of every six people in the city, according to a 1993 survey by the Santa Fe Arts Commission. The Santa Fe Indian Market, held annually in August, attracts over 100,000 visitors for this week-end event, dwarfing the city's resident population of approximately 63,500.

An "Arts and Economics Prosperity" study conducted in 2000–2001 by Americans for Advancing the Arts in America, the nation's leading nonprofit organization for supporting the arts in America, estimated that the nonprofit arts alone in Santa Fe are a 222.6-million-dollar industry supporting business development and jobs, and generating government revenue for the city.

Historical tourism emphasizes "historical sites, remains, replicas, and reenactments where the past is still being lived in and/or set off as a commercial entity" (Lippard, 1999, p. 72). Prime examples of these types of venues in Santa Fe include the downtown Palace of the Governors, built in 1610 and now a historical museum; El Rancho de las Golondrinas, a living history museum that reflects eighteenth-century Spanish colonial life; and the Santa Fe Fiesta, which is highlighted by a reenactment of the reconquest of Santa Fe by the Spaniards in 1692.

The final element in Lippard's cultural tourism is what she referred to as "ethnotourism," in which the flavor of the native culture is appropriated to give added color and spice to local art, products, and venues such as restaurants and lodging establishments. Examples of ethnotourism in Santa Fe range from the naming and decoration of local restaurants and hotels like La Fonda Hotel, near the Santa Fe Plaza, or the Pink Adobe Restaurant to the countless tourist souvenirs and collectibles sold in the shops lining the Plaza (Figure 1). The phenomenon of cultural tourism is not uncommon and certainly is not unique to Santa Fe. Many tourist destinations in the United States and beyond are particularly appealing to visitors because of the

Figure 1. La Fonda Hotel, 1985. The La Fonda is a popular hotel in downtown Santa Fe that emphasizes Spanish Colonial architecture and decoration as attractions for visitors. Photo by Carl Sheppard, Courtesy the Museum of New Mexico, #130966.

ambiance and flavor provided by the native population. However, indigenous cultures are more than just pleasant backdrops for vacationers, or commodities to be exploited financially by entrepreneurs. Culture exists outside the domains of tourism and commerce. At times, however, the line that separates authentic culture from commercial culture can become blurred.

Chris Wilson (1997), in his comprehensive examination of the creation and development of Santa Fe's architectural image, *The Myth of Santa Fe*, stated that "in a world infatuated with maintaining historical traditions and ethnic identities, Santa Fe has created an unusually successful illusion of authenticity" (p. 4). He referred to Santa Fe as an extreme example of what he calls the "invention of tradition." Wilson defined invented traditions as "reworking serviceable fragments from regional, family, and ethnic traditions, mixed with borrowings from other times and peoples, and leavened by pure invention." He stated that invented traditions frequently are "clothed in historical garb; they deny their origins while claiming historical authenticity" (p. 4). Wilson particularly focused on the use of "adobe style" architecture in Santa Fe to create the illusion that the city remained rooted in its traditional past.

In examining the historical evolution of Santa Fe and its impact on the city today, one can find numerous examples of how past events and inter-actions have been reinterpreted and/or reinvented for various purposes. Historical revisionism and social constructionism[1] have played a large part in creating the Santa Fe image that exists today.

Santa Fe has gone through a number of dramatic changes in recent years. The economy and lifestyle have been strongly affected by these social changes. Tourism now fuels the Santa Fe economy. City lodger's taxes bring in close to 5.5 million dollars a year and gross receipts from hotels tally over 100 million dollars annually. Santa Fe's total retail sales now top 1.6 billion dollars annually.

Art in Santa Fe is also a very big business, a type of commerce closely linked to tourism. In 1993, when the most recent comprehensive study of the Santa Fe art scene was conducted, it was estimated that art-related commerce accounted for 662.8 million dollars. Most art galleries reported that 75 to 80 percent of all sales were made to nonresidents (Stieber, 1998).

Santa Fe also benefits greatly from its status as the state capital of New Mexico. Government employment is a vital part of the city's economy. Federal, state, city, and county government account for over twenty-five thousand jobs in the Santa Fe area. These jobs provide a steady income and generous retirement packages for many locals.

Despite such prosperity, a variety of social problems exist in Santa Fe. Native Santa Feans find it difficult to afford to live in their own city. During the fourth quarter of 2002, the median cost of a house hit an all-time high in Santa Fe at $272,000. This price was a stunning $50,000 increase over the prior two years. Home ownership is virtually impossible for many current residents. Sharron Welsh, Director of Santa Fe Community Housing Trust, called affordable housing, a "chronic prob-lem" in the city (Quick, 1999).

The Santa Fe public education system is also a source of much concern to many residents. Santa Fe has a high school dropout rate that has ranged from 7.6 percent to 14.3 percent during the past ten years. Reasons for the poor educational record have been attributed to a lack of school funding, low teacher salaries, and a lack of meaningful employment opportunities in the community for high school graduates.

Santa Fe's population continues to grow. The city's population increased from about 20,000 in 1945, to 41,167 in 1970, to an estimated 63,500 in 2002. Long-term issues such as adequate water resources and quality of life are major concerns. Another major demographic change is that since the 1990 census, for the first time in the city's long history, non-Hispanics have achieved approximate parity with the Hispanic population. Hispanics made up 47.8 percent of the city's population according to the 2000 census.

It is in this context that Santa Fe's Hispanic people attempt to define their cultural self-identity. The focus of this book is to understand how outside influences have affected Hispanic cultural identity, and how this identity is being altered and maintained, and to examine the development of Hispanic cultural self-identity in Santa Fe. The impacts of tourism are also analyzed as to how they influence this self-identity. A key question is: When a culture is defined, interpreted, and/or commodified by an outside system for its vested interests, are natives of that culture influenced by this interpretation? Is this definition integrated into their cultural self-identity?

These issues are not only relevant to Santa Fe's Hispanic people, but are important to residents of cities around the world who find their environment and way of life increasingly commercialized for the sake of tourism and other enterprises. The issue of outside commodification[2] of a system is an essential part of global culture, which is encouraged by improved transportation and communication technology.

A review of existing publications revealed several works focusing on Santa Fe from a historical perspective and an even larger number of tourist-oriented publications, such as the Frommer's or Compass guide books, approaching the city as a romantic tourist haven. The thread running through many of these works was that they were written from an outsider's perspective, for nonresident readers. They were written from the outside looking into the system, examining the city of Santa Fe as a romantic place to visit or to study, but not representing the city or its local culture from an insider's point of view. An example of this difference in perception is the tendency to portray Santa Fe Hispanos as having a quaint, passive culture, frozen in the past and with the predilection of putting off difficult tasks until "*mañana.*" This simplification of the culture would be disputed by many Hispanic Santa Feans who see their culture and society as dynamic and contemporary.

I explore the insider's perspective of Santa Fe Hispanic culture for several reasons. First, I am a native Hispanic Santa Fean and a lifelong resident of the city. I often feel a disparity between the way I experience my cultural identity and the way I see it portrayed. This division in perceptions has been a source of confusion to me at times, and I am interested in how others in my culture have processed these seeming contradictions.

I approach these questions as a descendent of the two cultures that have occupied Santa Fe for the longest period of time. My ancestry includes a mixture of Spanish and Indian blood. I can trace roots to Spanish explorers, as well as to a grandfather from San Ildefonso Pueblo. Several labels have been used to describe this cultural blend over the years, including *"Mestizo," "Chicano," "Coyote," "Hispanic,"* and *"Latino."* These many titles suggest a variety of perspectives regarding cultural identification. These various terms have sprung from both "self-identification" and/or outside or "other-identification" sources.

CHAPTER TWO

Santa Fe Historical Background

In order to explore the question of how the diverse history of Santa Fe has influenced the cultural identity of Hispanic Santa Feans, it is imperative to look at the historical evolution of Santa Fe. A culture is the sum total of its past and present and does not spring from a void. My purpose is not to rewrite Santa Fe's history, but rather to provide a background for the examination of local Hispanic cultural identity. As such, it is a snapshot of a complex history that continues to unfold.

ANASAZI PERIOD

The original inhabitants of the area now known as Santa Fe were the Anasazi ("the ancient ones"), the ancestors of the Pueblo Indians who currently make up the nineteen reservations that exist in western and northern New Mexico (Sherman, 1996). These settlements are believed to have established several pueblo sites in the Santa Fe area prior to the Spanish arrival in the early 1600s.

Anasazi settlements along the Santa Fe River appear to have been developed as early as 1050 A.D. Archaeologists speculate that several large villages were established during what is termed the "Coalition Period" between 1175 and 1325, when the Anasazi joined with local indigenous peoples in developing communities in the Santa Fe area (Wilson, 1997).

Between 1415 and 1425, the Santa Fe region experienced one of its worst droughts in centuries, and many local villages were abandoned. When the Spanish arrived from 1607 to 1610, these once-thriving Pueblo villages had been abandoned for two hundred years (Sherman, 1996).

THE BEGINNING OF SPANISH EXPANSIONISM

Spain was at the forefront of European exploration of the Americas in the late 1400s and early 1500s. As one of the strongest and wealthiest nations in Europe, Spain was anxious to claim as much of the New World as possible before its rivals, France and England, got a foothold in these new lands (Perrigo, 1971).

Initially, the main motivation for Spain's interest in traveling to the New World was the desire to discover a trade route to the Far East. When Columbus's expedition was funded by King Ferdinand and Queen Isabella of Spain, this objective was one of the ultimate goals for the voyage. Also, medieval legends described in ancient Spanish literature fueled a belief that fabulous places existed in these faraway lands, filled with unknown riches and resources (Simmons, 1988).

The Spain of this expansionist period was a united country with a stable leadership. The Spaniards who were preparing to colonize the Americas had other attributes that would radically influence the way they acted during their future excursions. The Spaniards had one of the oldest and most diverse heritages in Europe, a country made up of many different backgrounds. They were descendants of the ancient Iberians who had in turn been invaded and mixed with the Carthaginians, Celts, Romans, Vandals, Visigoths, and Moors. The migration and cultural contributions of Jews, particularly from the south, added to the Spanish cultural mix. Thus, it was difficult even then to define a "typical" Spaniard. Spain of 1492 could then be divided into five regions: Castile, Andalusia, Galicia, the Basque country, and Catalonia, each of which was unique and each of which later sent explorers and settlers to the New World (Novas, 1994). Carlos Fuentes (1992) wrote that Latino descendants of the Spanish explorers are true racial and ethnic mixtures. Not only are many modern Hispanics mestizos, possible combinations of European, Indian, and African blood, but if we go back to their Spanish heritage, we may find an Iberian, Greek, Roman, Jewish, Arab, Gothic, and/or Gypsy heritage.

Another aspect of Spanish culture during this period that influenced the Spanish conquest was a single-minded belief in Christian conversion and domination. The racial and ethnic mingling of the Spanish culture did not extend to religious belief. The Spanish Inquisition in 1483 presided over by a high council and Tomás de Torquemada, the Grand Inquisitor, was endorsed by King Ferdinand and Queen Isabella and by Pope Sixus IV. The use of torture, mass burning, and cultural destruction was considered appropriate in waging war for the Christian cause (Novas, 1994). The conquerors of the New World were "a part of this reality," according to Fuentes (1992, p. 88). This religious intolerance (widespread throughout Europe at the time) and the zeal to convert by any means possible was a well-documented characteristic of the Spanish colonizers of the Americas.

The establishment of Spanish footholds in Havana and in other Caribbean ports in 1493 led to trips by Ponce de León in 1513 to Florida and by Cortés to Mexico in 1519 to conquer the Aztec Empire.

In two years, Cortés defeated the Aztecs and claimed Mexico for the Spanish Empire. From the new Spanish capital in Mexico City, the Spanish conquistadors began to expand north and south. This exploration and expansion quickly reached the northern frontier of New Spain and spread into what would later become the American Southwest (Perrigo, 1971).

SPANISH EXPLORATION AND COLONIZATION IN THE SOUTHWEST

In 1540, Francisco Vásquez de Coronado led a Spanish expedition north from present Mexico into what is now the American Southwest. This initial foray would blaze the trail for the eventual colonization of Santa Fe approximately seventy years later.

Although Coronado did not accomplish his intended goal of finding gold and other mineral riches, he did lay the foundation for the future exploration of the northern frontier of Spanish Mexico. Coronado passed within a few miles of present-day Santa Fe in his search for the legendary Seven Cities of Cibola, believed to be cities of gold dwarfing the riches that the Spaniards had plundered from the Aztec and Inca civilizations. Coronado eventually traveled as far north as Kansas before giving up his quest and returning to Mexico.

In 1598, a major Spanish expedition into New Mexico was led by Juan de Oñate. Oñate's expedition differed from Coronado's in one major respect. Oñate came north to colonize the frontier as well as to look for riches. He brought a troop of over 600 people including 11 Franciscan friars and 130 soldiers and their families.

Oñate established the first permanent European colony in New Mexico at present-day San Juan Pueblo, thirty miles north of Santa Fe.

The Spanish settlers were received with courtesy and generosity by the San Juan Indians. It is said that the San Juan people even offered some of their homes on the west side of the river to the Spaniards. The Spaniards came to call the Pueblo "San Juan de los Caballeros" as a tribute to this hospitality (Coan, 1925). The colony was later renamed San Gabriel. Life was harsh for the settlers and when the reality set in that instead of easy wealth, life in this northern frontier would consist of only meager subsistence, many of the pioneers returned to Mexico. Oñate resigned his governor's post in 1607 after being convicted of twelve offenses mainly related to the use of excessive force with the Acoma Indians and his own soldiers during his governorship. In 1610, Oñate was replaced by Pedro de Peralta, who along with a new group of colonists and the remaining settlers from San Gabriel established the new capital of Santa Fe (Simmons, 1991).

The nature of early Spanish colonization in New Mexico has been extensively debated. Some historical accounts, often produced as public relations pieces or for tourist consumption, paint a picture of a harmonious blending of cultures that resulted in the multicultural Santa Fe that exists today. Other accounts emphasize the barbarous nature of the Spanish conquistadors and fail to place the events in the perspective of the times in which they occurred. In either case, it is important to keep in mind that historical events are subject to interpretation so that historical "facts" often differ according to the perspective of the researcher.

Historical records cite that on July 7, 1540, Coronado's soldiers approached the Zuni Pueblo of Hawikuh expecting to find one of the legendary Seven Cities of Cibola. To their disappointment, they found only a poor, mud village. A skirmish ensued in which the overmatched Zuni people were overtaken and many were killed. Later, Coronado was personally charged with abusing the population in violation of the Spanish Law of the Indies, which decreed "friendly relations with native peoples." Although Coronado was eventually acquitted, he was implicated in a massacre of the village of Tiquex, near present-day Albuquerque, in which Spanish troops were reported to have burned thirty Indian rebels at the stake.

Oñate's reputation was also tarnished by a reported incident at Acoma Pueblo in 1598. In an ambush of Acoma warriors, thirteen Spaniards were killed. In retaliation, Oñate sent seventy Spanish soldiers and artillery to this high mesa pueblo and exacted a revenge that left only six hundred survivors from an estimated population of two thousand. The pueblo was set on fire and hundreds were killed when they were trapped or leaped from the cliffs. Many Acoma prisoners received harsh treatment. Children under the age of twelve became servants of the missionaries and soldiers, older Acoma were sentenced to twenty years of servitude (Twitchell, 1911). This treatment of the Acoma enticed criticism from Spanish authorities that felt Oñate had violated the spirit of the Law of the Indies. Eventually this incident contributed to Oñate's return to Mexico.

To this day, Oñate's actions at Acoma are often cited when critics of Spanish colonization voice concerns. In a 1999 incident that highlights the lingering resentment over Oñate's treatment of the Acoma, a bronze statue of Oñate was defaced by unknown assailants near the city of Española, New Mexico. A foot was cut off from a bronze likeness of Oñate that stood as a monument to the Spanish leader. This action was likely in response to the story that was told of Oñate ordering one foot cut off from several Acoma men after the 1598 ambush. The accuracy of this chopped-foot story is still under question.

Another controversy surrounding the Spanish colonization of New Mexico was the "encomienda" system. This arrangement required Pueblo Indians to provide basic provisions to the Spaniards, such as food and blankets, in exchange for Christian education and protection. This system put a great deal of strain on the Pueblos, especially during times of drought and because of the dwindling native population, due in part to diseases such as smallpox and influenza introduced by the Spanish. Often Pueblo people suffered starvation and severe hardships attempting to produce the required tribute mandated under the encomienda system.

The impact of Spanish colonization on Pueblo Indian life was in many ways devastating. However, it would be an oversimplification to characterize Spanish motivations as being entirely exploitative in nature. The Spanish Law of the Indies, developed by King Philip II of Spain in 1573, decreed that Spanish colonization should not damage native populations and mandated that colonists maintain good relations with native inhabitants (Wilson, 1997). Although the eventual implementation of these ideals fell considerably short of these intentions, much of the Spanish resources were directed toward building approximately fifty mission churches in Indian pueblos during the 1600s. From the Spanish point of view, an important motivation for the colonization of the northern frontier was to spread Christianity to the native population and to educate the native residents in how to live a less "primitive" life.

THE PUEBLO REVOLT

The Pueblo Indian people became more and more disenchanted with Spanish rule, and as early as 1650 Puebloans were plotting eventual revolt against the Spanish presence. The severe punishment and discipline that the Spanish imposed on the Indian population mirrored the treatment of Spanish subjects in Iberia under the reign of the Spanish Inquisition. The Pueblo people were unhappy with the exhaustive demands of providing resources for the Spanish under the encomienda system, the devastating diseases that reduced their population, and the repression of their native religions and customs.

Ramon A. Gutiérrez (1991) contended that many Spanish sojourns into Pueblo Indian territory were justified as waging a "just war" but in reality were expeditions to obtain slave labor. By 1680, half of all Spanish households owned slaves, with many having multiple Indian servants. According to Gutiérrez (1991), even the ascetic friars possessed personal slaves.

Even though Spanish-Indian relations included a high degree of intermarriage and cultural intermingling, these ties were not strong enough to prevent the Pueblo Revolt of 1680.

On August 11, 1680, the Revolt began, led by a Tewa warrior named Popé. The Spanish colonists were driven from their capital of Santa Fe, short of food and water and outnumbered in battle. They deserted the Palace of the Governors and retreated about three hundred miles south to El Paso del Norte, near present-day Ciudad Juárez, Mexico where they remained in exile for the next thirteen years (Simmons, 1988).

SPANISH RECONQUEST

During the period that the Pueblo Indians occupied Santa Fe after the Pueblo Revolt, two thousand Spanish settlers waited impatiently for an appropriate time to reclaim Santa Fe. In 1692, the Spanish governor in exile, Don Diego de Vargas, led an expedition to the former capital. In the predawn darkness of Saturday, September 13, he approached the fields surrounding the Palace stronghold on the Santa Fe Plaza with forty mounted soldiers, sixty Spanish subjects, Indian auxiliaries, and two Franciscan friars (Kessell, 1989).

De Vargas announced to the Pueblo inhabitants that he had come to pardon them and accept their obedience to God and king. The results were predictable. He was met with defiance and curses. To reinforce his resolve, De Vargas displayed a small cannon and mortar and cut off the ditch supplying water to the fortress. Negotiations dragged on from early that morning until late in the afternoon. Finally, De Vargas's "diplomacy" convinced the native leaders to make peace.

The next day, the Franciscans celebrated mass and absolved the wary Pueblo leaders. In another act of ritual conquest, De Vargas had dozens of Indian children baptized who had been born following the 1680 revolt (Kessell, 1989).

The question frequently asked by historians examining this "bloodless" reconquest of Santa Fe in 1692 relates to the Pueblo leaders' understanding of the rituals the Spanish were performing. Did the Pueblo leaders recognize the difference between ritual repossession and actual occupation during De Vargas's 1692 visit to Santa Fe?

Although the events of 1692 were celebrated in Mexico soon afterward as a peaceful reconquest (documented by Mexican scholar Sigüenza y Góngora under the title "Mercuio Volante") and continue to be celebrated as such in Santa Fe's annual Fiesta, there is evidence that supports a quite different interpretation by the Puebloans of the 1692 events.

De Vargas returned to El Paso in December 1692, to prepare for a permanent resettlement of Santa Fe. He then returned to Santa Fe in October 1693, with seventy families and a contingent of soldiers to reclaim the northern Spanish capital. However, events did not proceed as smoothly as De Vargas had anticipated. Winter came early to Santa Fe and provisions ran low as the Spaniards approached the city. The Pueblo people were not eager to abandon the houses and buildings they had occupied since the Revolt or to share food and other provisions with the hungry, freezing Spaniards who camped in the fields on the outskirts of the Santa Fe Plaza. De Vargas unsuccessfully tried to gain peaceful entry into the city while his contingent suffered and grew increasingly impatient. While camped outside the city, the Spaniards suffered through two blizzards in which twenty-two children under the age of sixteen died.

Finally, on December 29, 1693, due to the inclement weather and complaints from his expedition, De Vargas decided to occupy some public buildings in the villa. In a hard-fought battle in which fighters from Pecos Pueblo joined the Spanish, the capital was recaptured. Twenty-one Spaniards and eighty-one Indians died in the battle. De Vargas ordered the execution of seventy Pueblo defenders, and he sentenced four hundred others to ten years of servitude (Kessell, 1979).

Many researchers consider this less-idealized second return of De Vargas as the true reconquest of Santa Fe. The interpretations of the events of 1692–1693 have been debated over the years, particularly in relation to Santa Fe's annual Fiesta celebration.

SPANISH RESETTLEMENT 1693–1821

Spanish colonial life in Santa Fe during the late 1600s and throughout the 1700s was a struggle for survival without amenities. The dreams of wealth and untapped riches had disappeared, and the reality of a marginal existence remained. The settlers were austere and practical in their daily affairs.

Santa Fe was a remote capital supported by farming and ranching homesteads that were spread across northern New Mexico (see Figure 2). A 1790 census counted a Santa Fe population of 2,542 and showed farming as the most common occupation in the area. Out of 564 total heads of households, 264 (46 percent) were listed as farmers. Another sixty workers were identified as day laborers that generally worked on local farms. The remainder of working Santa Feans contributed to the self-sufficient society through their labor as adobe makers, carpenters, blacksmiths, weavers, etc. Interestingly, the 1790 census lists only one schoolteacher. Literacy was the exception, seen as an unnecessary luxury (Bustamante, 1989).

The fourteen-hundred-mile distance between Santa Fe and Mexico City hampered trade and communication with Mexico. Goods were mostly handmade out of necessity. Local trading with natives in Taos and Pecos provided some additional bartering opportunities for Santa Feans. Little money was circulated during this time.

Feast days, Christmas, and weddings were the social events that brought

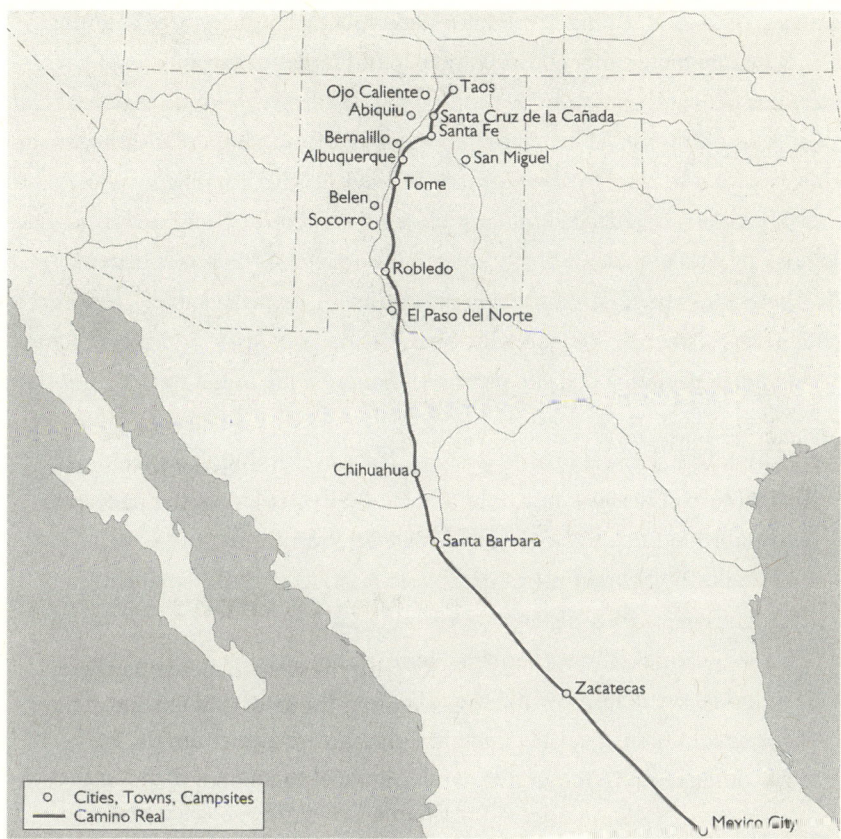

Figure 2. Map of Mexico/New Mexico Region, Spanish Colonial Period. The 1,400-mile trek between the Spanish capital in Mexico City and Santa Fe made contact infrequent and led to the development of a unique Santa Fe colonial culture. From Simmons (1998, p. 89). Used by permission of the University of New Mexico Press.

the community together. The yearly cleaning of irrigation ditches, or *acequias*, was also an important social event as well as a practical necessity.

During the late eighteenth century, a religious community who deemed themselves the "Brotherhood of Our Father Jesus" developed in northern New Mexico. They were a lay religious society of the Roman Catholic Church who came to be known as the *Penitente* Brotherhood. Penitente groups came into being in several Hispanic communities in northern New Mexico and southern Colorado. The Penitentes provided spiritual and civic guidance to the Spanish settlers. The scarcity of priests in the region required these Penitente groups to provide a variety of services and functions for the settlers, such as presiding at weddings and funerals and settling disputes.

The Penitente order consisted of men of Hispanic descent who had strong religious faith and who were committed to providing charity and mutual aid to their fellow colonists. They gathered in places of worship called *moradas*, and they were led by the *Hermano Mayor* or "elder brother" (Weigle, 1976).

Historians have traced the Penitente movement in New Mexico to similar groups who practiced shortly after the conquest of Mexico. These Mexican brotherhoods are believed to have derived from "confraternities" founded in the early sixteenth century in Spain (Shalkop, 1967). Friar Anancio Dominguez painted a realistic picture of Santa Fe life in his 1776 description:

> This villa . . . in the final analysis . . . lacks everything. Its appearance is mournful because not only are the houses of earth, but they are not adorned by any artifice of brush or construction. To conclude, the villa of Santa Fe (for the most part) consists of many small ranches at various distances from one another, with no plan as to their locations, for each owner built as he was able, wished to, or found convenient, now for the little farms they have there, now for the small herds of cattle which they keep in corrals of stakes, or else for other reasons. (cited in Adams and Chavez, 1956, pp. 39–40)

Spanish society during the colonial period from 1693 through 1821 was stratified by a system of ethnic categorization in which social status was determined by racial ancestry. This method of social hierarchy has come to be referred to as the "casta" system. The term *casta* was used to describe people with mixed ancestry in eighteenth-century Santa Fe who were not "*Españoles*" (people with pure Spanish blood). One's social standing was determined by the degree of "*pureza de sangre Española*" that one possessed (Bustamante, 1989).

A complex system developed to attempt to categorize the multiple combinations of ethnicities that were created by the interactions and inter-marriages of the inhabitants of New Mexico. Multiple labels were created to describe people of different racial combinations. At the top of the racial hierarchy were the "Españoles." This category usually included the wealthy Spanish aristocracy of the region.

Below the "Españoles" on the social ladder were the "mestizos" of mixed Spanish and Indian blood. The term *coyote* seems to have been used interchangeably with "mestizo," although it appears "coyote" often was used to refer to darker-skinned "mestizos."

Genízaro was a term used to describe full-blooded Indians who were captured at a young age by warring Plains Indians and sold to Spanish colonists as servants. These Indians took the name of the Spanish households, in which they worked and were raised, speaking Spanish and practicing Christianity. Census takers described "genízaros" as civilized Indians who were not Pueblo (Bustamante, 1989).

At the bottom of the *casta* system were the "*indios*" or Pueblo Indians who lived in the neighboring pueblos (Wilson, 1997).

A variety of other, more detailed categorizations within these major classifications divided ethnic differences even further. It was possible to raise one's status to a higher "casta" level if one had adequate social or economic power. Social differentiation was often more of a determining factor than ethnicity. Bustamante (1989) wrote that the high numbers of "Españoles" reported in the 1790 census of Santa Fe indicated that some residents classified as "Españoles" were in reality "mestizos" who had earned enough distinction politically and/or financially to pass as "Españoles." Bustamante speculated that other "casta" groups might have striven for a higher social ranking as well.

THE SANTA FE MEXICAN PERIOD

The year 1821 was pivotal in Santa Fe history. That year, the Mexican government declared independence from Spain. The battle for Mexican independence was an immense struggle in which 600,000 lives were lost. However, the residents of Santa Fe were far removed from the upheaval. The war for independence was fought entirely in today's Mexico (Sherman, 1996). Being over a thousand miles away from the center of the independence movement, the people of Santa Fe did not even hear of the new Mexican government until several months after the fact, when mail arrived informing the local governor that he must take an oath of allegiance to the new government. Other than that, nothing much changed for the relatively isolated colony (LeCompte, 1989).

The Mexican government was in constant turmoil during its early years. It had little time or resources to deal with its outpost in distant Santa Fe. The Mexican presidency changed twenty-seven times between 1821 and 1837.

Church influence was also minimal during the Mexican period. Priests were scarce and religious sacraments were neglected. Only five to eight priests remained in New Mexico during this time. Soon after Mexico gained independence, most natives of Spain, which included most of the Franciscans, were banished from Mexican soil.

No bishops visited the Santa Fe area between 1760 and 1832, although Bishop Zubiría from Durango did manage three visits after 1833. Confirmations were rare, baptism decreased, and many couples lived together without formal marriages. More and more, Santa Feans looked toward the Penitentes to provide spiritual and civic leadership and guidance.

A major change that occurred during the Mexican period was the abolishment of the "casta" system. The old terminology was discouraged, as everyone was to be referred to as a "*Mexicano*" and held the title of "*don*" or "*doña*." The Mexican Constitution, modeled after the U.S. Constitution, also gave formal citizenship to both Indians and African descendants in the region (LeCompte, 1989).

Another change that eventually had a far-reaching impact on Santa Fe was the new openness of the Mexican government to allow trade with the United States. The Santa Fe Trail between Santa Fe and Independence, Missouri, was established in 1821 (see Figure 3). Santa Fe was to become a hub when the Santa Fe Trail connected to the Chihuahua Trail (Camino Real) and Old Spanish Trail.

Before the arrival of U.S. traders, Santa Feans were mainly self-reliant. However, American-made goods soon had an irreversible impact on Santa Fe lifestyles. The trade on the Santa Fe Trail transformed the material desires of the residents of Santa Fe. The goods that came to Santa Fe via the Santa Fe Trail were valuable resources for Santa Feans who traded with their neighbors to the south in present-day Chihuahua and Durango. American goods were coveted as valuable trading commodities.

Historian Janet LeCompte (1989) wrote, "A profusion of American mirrors appeared on the previously bare white-washed walls. For special occasions, women put aside their peasant blouses and skirts to appear at

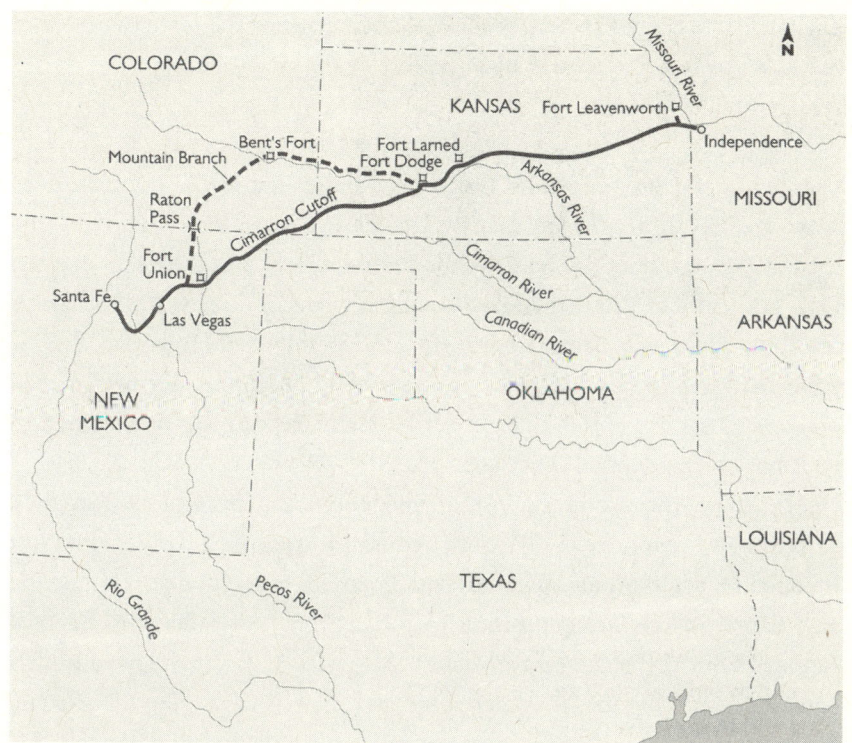

Figure 3. Map of Santa Fe Trail. The Santa Fe Trail, which extended from Independence, Missouri, to Santa Fe, brought an abundance of eastern U.S. goods to Santa Fe and influenced the tastes and culture of Hispanic Santa Feans. From Simmons (1998, p. 124). Used by permission of the University of New Mexico Press

halls in tight waisted American gowns" (p. 84).

Santa Fe women also reveled in their new-found freedoms. LeCompte (1989) wrote, "In an era when most wives of the world were mere chattels of their husbands, married women of Santa Fe kept their own wages and their maiden names. Their legal rights were such that they could even sue their husbands" (p. 86).

The most well-known woman in Santa Fe during this time was Gertrudes Barcelo, more widely known as "La Tules" ("Tules" was an affectionate nickname analogous to "Trudy" with "La" signifying a popular celebrity). She was the principal operator of a bar and gambling casino located in the part of Santa Fe now known as Burro Alley. She was also an expert card dealer. She was known far and wide as being fashionable, intelligent, and charming. She ran her establishment during the 1830s and 1840s and was so financially successful that after the U.S. occupation, she loaned money to the U.S. Army to help meet its payroll (LeCompte, 1989).

U.S. OCCUPATION

Conflict between Mexico and the United States led to the occupation of New Mexico in 1846. The tensions leading to war were fueled by the granting of statehood to Texas by the United States and the debts that the U.S. government claimed Mexico owed American citizens for lost assets resulting from the Mexican war for independence. However, a clear underlying factor was the American belief in "manifest destiny," which presumed that the territory west to the Pacific Ocean was predestined to be American controlled (Perrigo, 1964).

In 1846, three hundred American troops led by Colonel Stephen Kearny and supported by one thousand mounted volunteers left Independence, Missouri, and marched 856 miles to Santa Fe to occupy the city. Santa Fe was in no position to mount much of a defense. Lack of support from the central government in Mexico had left the local militia depleted. Knowing that they were no match for the advancing U.S. forces, Governor Armijo and many other Santa Feans decided to flee Santa Fe. On August 18, 1846, Kearney marched into Santa Fe unopposed. Not a drop of blood was spilled in the occupation. Tensions surfaced soon after the occupation, which led to an attempted uprising. Some Santa Fe leaders, who saw their influence diminish, decided to drive the Americans out of the territory. The plan was discovered, and a number of plotters were arrested. However, two of the rebel leaders, Tomás Ortiz and Colonel Diego Archuleta, escaped. They led an ambush a couple of weeks later, in which the new U.S. governor of the territory and five other officials were killed. The resistance spread; several more Americans were killed at Turley's Mill, north of Taos, and two traders were shot in Mora.

American retribution was swift and brutal. U.S. troops trapped the rebels in a church at Taos Pueblo. Artillery was used to destroy the church and approximately one hundred were killed in the church, and later as survivors fled to the surrounding mountains the U.S. Cavalry attacked them and another fifty were killed. Later, some twenty-five to thirty rebels were tried by court-martial for the uprising and sentenced to death

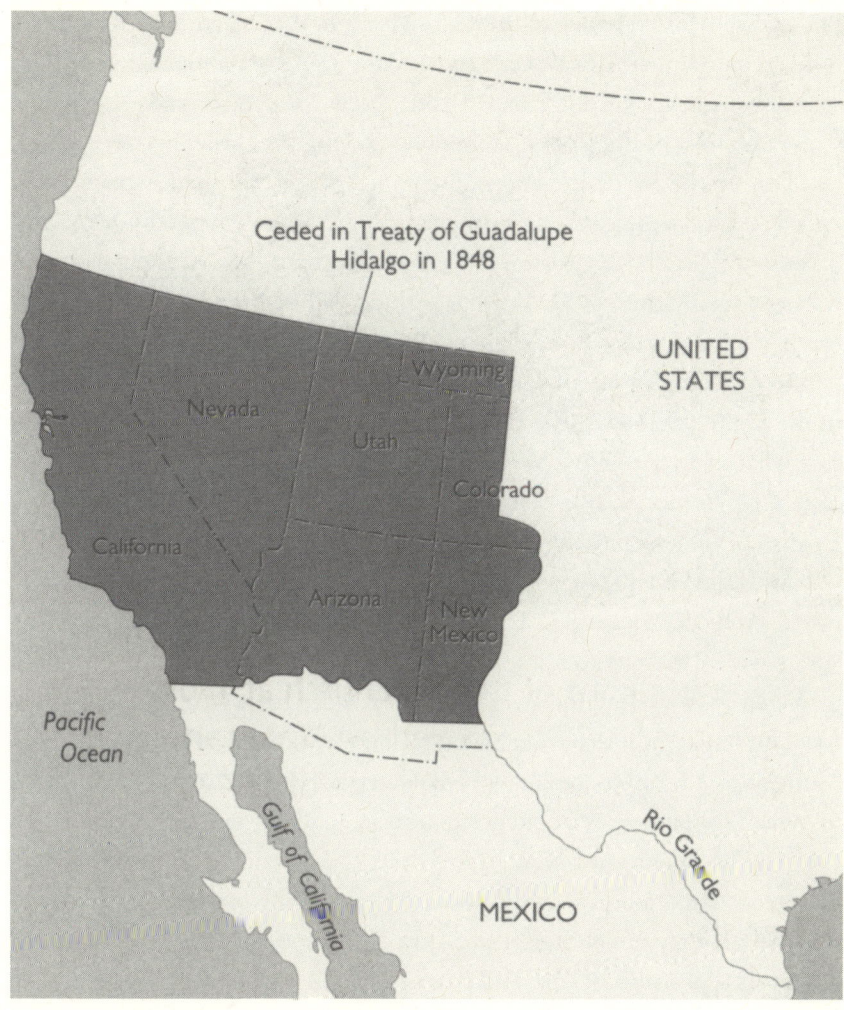

Figure 4. Map of Treaty of Guadalupe Hidalgo. On February 2, 1848, the Treaty of Guadalupe Hidalgo was signed by the U.S. and Mexico following the war. The Treaty required. Mexico to cede to the U.S. territory that now consists of much of the American Southwest. From Simmons (1998, p. 142). Used by permission of the University of New Mexico Press.

(Twitchell, 1912). Several were tried on treason charges that were controversial, since the prisoners were not citizens of the government they were being tried for treason against (Coan, 1925). In Mora, American soldiers retaliated for the murder of the traders by burning every building in the village (Wilson, 1989).

The signing of a peace treaty on February 2, 1848, at Guadalupe

Hidalgo in Mexico brought the U.S.-Mexican War to an end. The treaty terms required that Mexico cede to the American government the territory that now comprises California, Arizona, New Mexico, Nevada, Utah, and Colorado, west of the Rocky Mountains (see Figure 4) (Perrigo, 1964).

During the 1850s and 1860s, the U.S. Army established a strong presence in New Mexico, setting up a garrison in Santa Fe named Fort Marcy. The New Mexico Territory was much larger then than present-day New Mexico. It stretched to California, included all of Arizona, and the western part of Colorado (Simmons, 1988).

In the compromise of 1850, Congress declared New Mexico a territory of the United States. At the time, members of the U.S. Congress were not sure what to do with New Mexico. They felt the territory was not worthy of statehood, based on the perception that New Mexicans did not speak English or understand U.S. laws or the voting process (Simmons, 1988).

Mexican War propaganda painted New Mexicans as an inferior race of mixed ethnicity, incapable of following democratic principles or of taking advantage of the territory's resources. The same prejudices that had been projected on blacks and Indians were now extended to those of Mexican ancestry. The single most determining factor in delaying statehood was that New Mexico was a Spanish-speaking, Catholic territory that easterners considered foreign. These attitudes would postpone statehood for over sixty years.

The designation of New Mexico as a U.S. territory opened the gates to a steady stream of Americans from the east. Many of them were disdainful of what they encountered in Santa Fe. American attitudes associated adobe (bricks made of dirt and straw) with lack of morals, hygiene, and civilization (see Figure 5) (Wilson, 1997).

Toward the latter part of the 1800s, there was a concerted effort to transform Santa Fe into what Oliver LaFarge described as a replica of "a minor Indiana town." Americans brought in milled posts and trim to create the illusion that the adobe buildings did not exist. They were partial to a simplified Greek revival style that is referred to locally today as "territorial" style (Wilson, 1997).

A classic example of this transformation is the St. Francis Cathedral Church. Between 1869 and 1886, Archbishop Lamy, who seemed to share the American dislike for local culture and architecture, began a massive effort to erect a Romanesque church to replace the adobe *parroquia* that had stood on the spot since 1714 (see Figure 6). Symbolically, he built the new church by surrounding the old structure with massive stone walls and then dismantled the old church adobe brick by adobe brick and had them carried out the new front doors. This architectural siege corresponded to his campaign to stamp out the local brand of folk Catholicism typified by the Penitentes.

French born, Jean Baptiste Lamy arrived in Santa Fe in 1851 when the Catholic churches in New Mexico were transferred from the Diocese of Durango, Mexico, to American control. Lamy was reassigned from Cincinnati, Ohio, to Santa Fe to run the new diocese. He was determined to transform Santa Fe Catholicism into a Franco-American model. He brought in foreign clergy from France, Belgium, and Italy to encourage a new style of Catholicism (Hammond and Donnelly, 1936).

Perhaps the single event that did the most to change the nature of the territory was the coming of the railroad in 1880. New people arrived by the thousands. Between 1880 and 1900, the Anglo population of New Mexico quadrupled. By 1886 Spanish-surnamed property ownership diminished by 48 percent (Wilson, 1997).

A new elite class developed in Santa Fe comprised of Anglo lawyers and territorial government officials. This informal coalition, which has been referred to as "The Santa Fe Ring," appropriated vast amounts of land during the late 1800s and early 1900s. By 1912 they had manipulated the judicial and legislative systems to such an extent that they controlled 80 percent of the former lands held by Mexican farmers and ranchers (Wilson, 1997).

CONTEMPORARY SANTA FE

The early twentieth century brought a renewed appreciation for the native architecture and lifestyle, reversing the earlier drive to "Americanize" Santa Fe. Whereas nineteenth-century Anglo-Americans considered Santa Fe backward and its appearance undesirable, newcomers in the early 1900s, many of whom were artists and anthropologists, saw Santa Fe style as aesthetic and even virtuous. New building was encouraged to reflect Spanish-Pueblo Revival style. This consistency in architecture came to be referred to as "Santa Fe style" (Sherman, 1996).

The catalyst for this shift in building preference came from the

Figure 5. 1881 Santa Fe Adobe Building. Photo by William H. Jackson. Courtesy the Museum of New Mexico, #10140.

influence of the Museum of New Mexico/School of American Archeology, founded in 1909. A plan put forward by the Museum called for the city to encourage more homogeneous new construction based on the Santa Fe style. Museum leaders felt the plan would help to set Santa Fe apart from other cities. Subsequently, the Chamber of Commerce coined the label "The City Different" to support this vision.

Santa Fe style was reflected in an exhibit developed for the 1914 San Diego Exposition. The New Mexico State Exposition Building was styled after mission churches at Acoma, Zia, and Laguna pueblos. The building was enthusiastically received and fueled interest in spreading the style throughout Santa Fe. Examples of buildings that were part of this revival movement during this period include the Museum of Fine Arts, the New Mexico School for the Deaf (see Figure 7), the Forest Service Building, and La Fonda Hotel (Wilson, 1997).

The prime motivating factor for the "City Different" movement was the perceived economic boost that tourism would bring to the area. Ironically, the city found itself "between a rock and a hard place" in trying to promote itself as a quaint, rustic village and, at the same time, the capital of a progressive territory vying for statehood.

Figure 6. St. Francis Cathedral, 1900. Photo by Rev. John C. Gullette. Courtesy the Museum of New Mexico, #13250.

The 1920s and 1930s was a time of gradual and sustained growth for Santa Fe. The Santa Fe Fiesta celebration, which was inactive between 1913 and 1918 due in part to World War I and local preoccupation with the 1914 San Diego Exposition, was revived in 1919 and developed under the auspices of the Museum of New Mexico. The city's population grew from 7,236 in 1920 to 11,176 in 1930, to over 20,325 in 1940. Even though changes occurred rapidly, Santa Fe and New Mexico still struggled to sustain their populations economically. A Works Progress Administration (WPA) survey in the late 1930s cited an average annual per capita income in northern New Mexico of thirty-seven dollars. Jobs were scarce and mainly unskilled in nature. A 1940 survey reported that 41.5 percent of habitable dwellings in New Mexico lacked running water (Kusel and Smith, 1999).

The coming of World War II had a dramatic impact on Santa Fe. Frank Rand, the owner of *The New Mexican*, Santa Fe's city newspaper, said in 1942 that the city was "awfully sick" after having lost 10 percent of its population to the draft and to war industries outside the state (Kusel and Smith, 1999). However, the war also brought new activity to the city. Bruns Hospital was built in Santa Fe in the early 1940s by the U.S. War Department as a military hospital. In 1945 it housed twenty-two hundred patients and was the town's largest employer, putting to work over one thousand local people.

Santa Fe also became the site of an internment camp for Japanese and Japanese-Americans relocated from the West Coast during World War II. Camp Santa Fe held a maximum of over 2,000 such prisoners between 1942 and 1946, with a total of 4,555 Japanese-Americans passing through the Santa Fe camp. The site was a former Civilian Conservation Corps camp, an area that has since become a housing subdivision on the west side of the city. The camp provided about 80 temporary guard jobs for Santa Feans (Wilson, 1997).

Santa Feans also felt the effects of a secret war project located fifteen miles north on the Pajarito Plateau. Hundreds of military personnel and scientists passed through Santa Fe on their way to the newly formed city of six thousand, soon known as Los Alamos, the home of the atomic bomb. However, the impact of the Manhattan Project at Los Alamos on Santa Fe was minimal, initially due to secrecy restrictions on Los Alamos residents at the time (Kusel and Smith, 1999).

The 1950s saw Santa Fe's continued growth and a return to its obsession with tourism. Art came to be a vital industry in the city and art galleries sprang up around the Plaza and along Canyon Road. The Santa Fe Opera opened in 1957, drawing performers and visitors from around the world. In the 1960s, tourism and government were the primary employers in Santa Fe. By the end of the 1970s, the city's population was almost fifty thousand (Sherman, 1996). In 2000 it had reached sixty-two thousand.

The Santa Fe Tourism Boom

The early 1980s were the beginning of the tourism explosion that transformed Santa Fe into an international destination. National magazine exposure announced to the world that Santa Fe was the "in" place to be. In 1981, *U.S. News and World Report* called Santa Fe "the new Palm Springs." *People* magazine labeled it "the sagebrush Shangri-La . . . a mecca of mesas and margaritas." A May 1981 *Esquire* article called Santa Fe "the best place to live in America."

Media attention led to a swelling of new tourism and an influx of wealthy new residents in the 1980s and 1990s. High-priced shops sprang up everywhere, while home and land prices in Santa Fe soared.

As Santa Fe became the "in" place to live, it began to attract a growing number of celebrities. Among the rich and famous who established

Figure 7. The New Mexico School for the Deaf, 1917. The New Mexico School for the Deaf was a classic example of the push in the early 1900s to use "Santa Fe style" adobe architecture to promote a unique image for Santa Fe. Courtesy the Museum of New Mexico, #50912.

homes in Santa Fe were George McGovern, former presidential nominee, and John Erlichmann, former Nixon White House official.

Film stars calling Santa Fe home included Amy Irving, Tab Hunter, Ali MacGraw, Ted Danson, Val Kilmer, Carol Burnett, Brian Dennehy, Shirley MacLaine, Oprah Winfrey, Jane Fonda, Robert Redford, Gene Hackman, and Marsha Mason. Musical celebrities making homes in Santa Fe have included James Taylor, Randy Travis, Roger Miller, and Herbie Mann.

Business leaders such as Calvin Klein, Ralph Lauren, and Stanley Marcus have also called Santa Fe home. Other well-known people who have lived in Santa Fe include artist Judy Chicago; Bill Watterson, creator of the comic strip "Calvin and Hobbes"; playwright Neil Simon; political cartoonists Bill Mauldin and Pat Oliphant; and Chuck Jones, animation director and founding father of many Warner Brothers Looney Tunes characters. In fact, so many celebrities have lived in and visited Santa Fe over the last twenty years that a popular column in the local newspaper *The Santa Fe New Mexican*, called *El Mitote*, reported celebrity sightings around the city.

In 1990, for the first time in the city's history, the Anglo population in Santa Fe outnumbered Hispanic residents. Santa Fe was becoming a place that was too expensive for most local people to live in. In a report produced by the

Table 1. Santa Fe Historical Timeline

DATE	EVENT
1175–1325	"Coalition Period." Several large Anasazi settlements established along the area of the Santa Fe River.
1415–1425	Drought leads Anasazi to abandon Santa Fe area village.
1540	Francisco Vásquez de Coronado leads a Spanish expedition that passes within a few miles of Santa Fe in his search for the "Seven Cities of Gold."
1598	Juan de Oñate establishes the first European colony in New Mexico thirty miles north of Santa Fe. In a battle with the Acoma Indians, eight hundred Acoma are killed and Oñate inflicts harsh sentences on the survivors.
1607	Village of Santa Fe is established.
1610	Oñate is replaced as governor by Pedro de Peralta, who establishes the capital of Santa Fe.
1680	Pueblo Revolt: The Spanish are driven from Santa Fe to El Paso del Norte. Pueblo Indians rule Santa Fe for the next thirteen years.
1692	Don Diego de Vargas leads a Spanish expedition into Santa Fe and negotiates a peace settlement with the Pueblo Indian occupants of Santa Fe before returning to El Paso del Norte.
1693	De Vargas returns to Santa Fe to resettle the city. After a two-week stand-off, the Spaniards take the city after a battle in which twenty-one Spaniards and eighty-one Indians are killed. De Vargas orders the execution of seventy other Pueblo fighters and four hundred more Pueblo Indians are sentenced to servitude.
1693–1821	Spanish resettle Santa Fe, establishing an agricultural colonial society.
1821	The Mexican government declares independence from Spain and Santa Fe becomes a part of a Mexican state. Also, the Santa Fe Trail is established between Santa Fe and Independence, Missouri.

city's Office of Community Development in the 1990s, it was estimated that Santa Fe's middle class was shrinking at the rate of 2 percent per year.

These changes led to a growing tension and a sense of loss for many Santa Feans. The election of Debbie Jaramillo as mayor of Santa Fe in 1994 reflected, at least in part, a growing concern that many residents felt about the direction in which their city was going.

Santa Fe continues to be a community at the crossroads, attempting to create a future that can accommodate change and also preserve the culture and integrity of its past.

DATE	EVENT
1846	On August 18, 1846, American troops occupy Santa Fe during the U.S.–Mexican War.
1848	The Treaty of Guadalupe Hidalgo is signed on February 2, 1848, ending the U.S. Mexican War. The treaty required Mexico to cede to the United States the territory that now compromises California, Arizona, New Mexico, Nevada, Utah, and part of Colorado.
1850	New Mexico is declared a territory of the United States.
1851	Reverend Jean Baptiste Lamy arrives in Santa Fe to oversee the Roman Catholic Church.
1862	Confederate forces capture Santa Fe for a brief period before being driven out by Union soldiers.
1880	Railroad spur to Santa Fe is completed bringing U.S. easterners by the thousands.
1880–1912	Through judicial and legislative manipulation, 80 percent of the lands around Santa Fe, formerly held by Mexican farmers and ranchers, are appropriated by lawyers, speculators, and territorial government officials.
1913–1940	Under the influence of the Museum of New Mexico, Santa Fe strives to portray itself as a tourist destination. During the 1920s and 1930s an art colony of Anglo artists from the eastern United States settles in Taos and Santa Fe.
1942–1946	During World War II, Santa Fe becomes the site of an internment camp for Japanese and Japanese-Americans, detaining 4,555 individuals.
1950–1980	Santa Fe's population grows from twenty-eight thousand to fifty thousand.
1980–2000	Santa Fe experiences a tourism explosion as the city gains a reputation as an international tourist destination. Tourism and development pressures become a source of concern to residents.

CHAPTER THREE

Santa Fe Hispanic Cultural Identity

HISTORICAL OVERVIEW OF
SANTA FE HISPANIC SELF-IDENTIFICATION

Insight into the cultural identity of Santa Fe Hispanics is provided by the labels that local Hispanics and others use in defining their ethnicity. Cultural labeling is a complex issue that has played an important role in Santa Fe cultural identification since before the city's Spanish founding in the seventeenth century.

A Spaniard who had traveled to the New World from Spain but who had been born in Spain was known as a *"Peninsular."* However, if he were born to the same parents in the New World, he was labeled a *"Criollo"* (Campa, 1979).

The casta system of ethnic and social stratification employed during the Spanish Colonial period in Santa Fe placed great emphasis on ancestral labels as a method for determining social status. "Españoles" (Spanish blood) were at the top of the social hierarchy, followed by "Mestizos" (mixed Spanish/Indian blood), and "Indios" (Pueblo Indians). Within these three basic categories were multiple subcategories that further delineated ancestry and social position.

The casta-system terminology gradually gave way to the designation of "Mexican" for the residents of Santa Fe and New Mexico after the Mexican Revolution of 1821, until the United States occupation twenty-five years later. However, it should be reiterated that the changes in governments from Spanish rule to Mexican Independence to U.S. occupation had a less dramatic impact on Santa Fe cultural identity than elsewhere because of the isolation of Santa Fe from the central governments. Santa Feans continued to go about their business as usual; they did not have time to become very political in their rural community.

The Mexican War gave rise to negative American stereotypes of anything related to Mexico and led to a shift from the racial designation of "Mexican" (actually a national designation) to "Spanish-American."

According to Campa (1979), the term *Spanish-American* served a triple purpose for New Mexicans after the U.S. occupation of the region. It distanced New Mexicans from the negative connotations associated with the label "Mexican," it transformed them into more exotic "Spaniards," and it reinforced their American citizenship.

In Santa Fe, the Museum of New Mexico encouraged the label "Spanish-American," believing that tourists would be more drawn to the image of Spanish *conquistadores* than images of working-class Mexicans epitomized and vilified by Pancho Villa. Santa Fe's political leaders also followed suit and began referring to themselves and their constituents as Spanish-Americans (Wilson, 1997).

The Santa Fe Hispanic *rico* elite (wealthy Santa Fe Hispanics) also emphasized their Spanish connection to express the common European roots that they shared with the Anglo-Americans with whom they shared power in the Santa Fe hierarchy. The implication was, in the local population's embrace of the term *Spanish-American*, that Santa Feans were not Mexican but were of pure Spanish ancestry without Indian blood. The label "Mexican" was at times used in New Mexico and the Southwest to refer to those people with darker skin, while the term *Spanish-American* was used to describe those with lighter skin (Campa, 1979).

The term *Chicano* was widely used by Mexican-American activists who participated in the Brown Power movement of the 1960s and 1970s in the southwestern United States. The term seems to have originated in the fields of California, where native Nahuatl speakers from Morelos had difficulty pronouncing the word *Mexicano* and instead called themselves "Mesheecanos." This became a slang term used to refer to darker-skinned Hispanics with close ties to Mexico (Chicano/LatinoNet.com, 2002).

The term *chicano* emphasized the underclass and underprivileged qualities and raised the formerly derogatory term to a status of pride. The chicano movement also acknowledged the Indian ancestry of people of Hispanic background (Campa, 1979). It served as an alternative perspective to the Spanish-American identity. The label "chicano" was never fully embraced by the Hispanic community and was most popular during the 1960s and 1970s.

The term *Hispanic*, or *Hispano*, is a relatively recent term that came into wider usage in the 1970s and 1980s. It has been the most commonly applied label to Spanish-speaking and Spanish-surnamed people in the United States, used widely in the media and by the U.S. government.

The label "Hispanic" classifies a population according to their ancestors' native language rather than by their culture, racial make-up, or geography. According to Novas (1994), the term *Hispanic* "encompasses no fewer than twenty-one separate republics, each with their own distinct culture and history, including indigenous languages, religions, foods, and individual philosophies" (p. 2).

The term *Hispanic* does not differentiate between the descendants of the Spanish conquerors, the Hispanicized Indians, Africans brought as slaves, or people from Mexico, Latin America, Cuba, or Puerto Rico. As Novas (1994) wrote, "you get the whole enchilada defined in the U.S. as Hispanic" (p. 2).

Criticism has been leveled against the term *Hispanic* by those who believe it homogenizes the culture that it represents and that the term does nothing more than set the group apart from Anglo-Americans and Indian Americans. Interestingly, in Latin America, which is the origin of many people referred to as Hispanic in the United States, no one refers to himself/herself as Hispanic. They identify themselves with their individual nationalities and cultures (such as "Cubans") (Novas, 1994). Proponents of the term *Hispanic* argue that the collective term unites Hispanics as a cultural group and gives its members more political and cultural influence.

The term *Latino*, which has gained popularity in recent years, has many of the strengths and weaknesses of the term *Hispanic*. The term generally includes people from North America, South America, and Central America who speak a language derived from Latin, mainly Spanish. However, it is so general that it does little to identify specific cultural groups within its wide spectrum. Numerous other terms have been introduced in the past and are currently used to refer to Hispanic New Mexicans and to Hispanics nationally. Reyes López Tijerina, a New Mexico land-grant advocate, promoted the term *Indio-Hispano*, and Cesar Chávez advocated a resurrection of "Mexican-American" but neither term caught on. Sometimes Hispanics use terms that reflect their regional affiliation such as *Texanos* or *Nuevo Mexicanos* (Campa, 1979). In Santa Fe, local terms such as *hermano*, *native*, or even *bro* are sometimes used to indicate Hispanic ethnic affiliation.

The complexity of Hispanic cultural labeling is reflected in the U.S. Census Bureau's 2000 questionnaire. Question no. 5 on the U.S. Census short form asks, "Is this person Spanish/Hispanic/Latino?" Under this heading people can choose between "Mexican/Mexican American or Chicano," "Puerto Rican," "Cuban," or "other Spanish/Hispanic/Latino." The next question, which asks informants to report their race, allows Hispanics yet another method of identifying themselves. If none of these categories are acceptable, respondents can write in their preference under the blank space titled "some other race" (Novak, 2000, March 6).

Defining Santa Fe Hispanic Cultural Identity

I interviewed a number of Santa Fe Hispanos and non-Hispanos to find out what their preferences were regarding cultural identifiers and how these terms reflect cultural identity. Additionally, I asked them to describe the specific elements that most defined and reflected Santa Fe Hispanic culture for them. In order to better understand Santa Fe Hispanic cultural identity, I also conducted a series of personal interviews with Santa Fe Hispanic cultural leaders and scholars. Briefer interviews were also conducted with a cross-section of Santa Feans (Hispanic and non-Hispanic). The intent of this data-gathering effort was to obtain a wide spectrum of perceptions about the nature of Santa Fe Hispanic culture and identity issues.

Roberto Mondragon

The first personal interview I conducted was with Roberto Mondragon. In addition to being the former lieutenant governor of New Mexico and a former Green Party candidate for governor of New Mexico, Mondragon, through his organization, "*Aspectos Culturales*," has been producing a bilingual monthly publication from Santa Fe called *Amigos* for over fourteen years. *Amigos* focuses on Hispanic history and culture in New Mexico and emphasizes reaching children in the public schools. In addition to this magazine, Mondragon broadcasts a biweekly radio program and produces publications and cassette tapes highlighting Hispanic culture and language.

Mondragon (2000) emphasized that it is important to look at Santa Fe

Hispanic culture in positive terms. He believed that the local Hispanic culture would continue to be preserved if Santa Fe Hispanos each did their share to maintain it. He warned about too much talk of "losing" the culture. He stated that instilling a sense of "accomplishment, pride and positive goals" in Santa Fe and New Mexican Hispanic students was the best way to preserve the culture.

Mondragon felt that New Mexico schools were not prepared to teach Hispanic history and culture to students. He stated, "When schools celebrate [Hispanic] culture, all they have is an enchilada dinner for Cinco de Mayo."

In characterizing Santa Fe Hispanic culture, Mondragon emphasized three key points. First, he stated that "Language is the soul of the culture" and that bilingual education was of central importance.[1]

Mondragon stated that "You can't talk about Santa Fe Hispanic culture without mentioning religion." Mondragon believed that the Catholic faith was also central in defining Santa Fe Hispano cultural identity. He stated that unlike local Hispanos, tourists might "buy a cross or a *santo*, or get a picture of a *Penitente*, but when they really see our religion they don't really understand it."

Third, Mondragon mentioned that Hispanics in New Mexico are a mixture of cultures. He commented that the richness of the local Hispanic culture comes not only from the mixture that took place in New Mexico, but even before that in Spain.

Mondragon's optimism about the future of Hispanic culture in Santa Fe and New Mexico was based on the amount of interest and effort that he observed. He cited organization such as the Sociedad Folklorica, the Hispanic Research Center in Albuquerque, acequia associations, the New Mexico Land Grant Forum, and ongoing bilingual school programs as examples of the preservation of Hispanic culture.

Orlando Romero

Orlando Romero is a New Mexican journalist and writer who has published numerous essays in journals, magazines, and newspapers relating to Hispano issues. He is the former director of the Fray Angelico Chávez History Library at the Palace of the Governors, located in downtown Santa Fe.

Romero (2000) warned about the misrepresentation of Hispano culture.

He stated that academic reporting of Hispanic culture can be a "false womb," quite different from reality. He was also concerned that the media's portrayal of Hispanics was "unrealistic." He stated, "In one paper, we're portrayed in a romantic way and in another, we're ignorant and backward."

Romero commented that the complexity of Santa Fe and New Mexican Hispanic culture was not easily defined. One factor, he noted, that made this culture unique was its distance and separation from Mexico in the past. He stated, "We developed a whole new sub-species, especially in the mountains of Northern New Mexico. The mountains were physical barriers that to some degree isolated people. As a result, New Mexico developed a different persona."

Romero also noted that New Mexico Hispanics could not deny their ancestral past, as in their roots from Spain. He said, "Many of the people who have written about us, want to lump us all together as Mexican-Americans or as the romantic Spanish-Americans. You get extreme contrasts."

Romero stated that cultural identity for Santa Fe Hispanics was difficult to assess. He commented,

> What does culture mean, eating at Taco Bell? Is it material things that make it? There are a lot of Hispanos who don't live in adobe houses, but Anglos do. There are a lot of Hispanos that no longer know how to clean an irrigation ditch or lay an adobe. Does that make him less Hispanic than you and I? What defines culture for a Hispano? (2000)

Romero echoed Roberto Mondragon's comments that Catholicism was at the core of the Santa Fe culture and Hispanic identity. He stated, "For me, [cultural identity] is being Catholic. If I couldn't go to communion, I just wouldn't want to live. That's how strongly I feel about my cultural connection to my church."

Romero (2000) cited the neighborly environment of Hispano culture. He elaborated:

> I have to surround myself with Latinos and hear Spanish spoken. I need to have Latinos who are passionate like me, who like to

have a nice glass of wine, like to dance, go to communion, and have a passion for life. Our music is so wonderful and rhythmic, and the food is hot and spicy like us. What defines culture? I think it's such a personalized, individual thing.

Romero believed that the demise of the local Hispanic culture was greatly exaggerated. He commented, "I think the culture is very much alive. The question about our culture dying has been asked since the 1800s when the Anglo culture conquered New Mexico. I think our culture is in transition." He added, "You have to not just look at the physical manifestations, you have to look at the spiritual energy of the Hispano people in the Santa Fe community. Thank God we're still close to 50 percent [of the Santa Fe population]."

With regard to cultural labels for Hispanos, Romero stated that he particularly liked the term *manito* because of its colloquial, regional characteristic. Manito is a derivative of "*hermanito*" or "*hermano*" which means "brother" in Spanish. Romero also said that he felt comfortable with *Hispano* as a term for cultural identification.

Ana Pacheco

Ana Pacheco (2000) started her Santa Fe publication *La Herencia* in the spring of 1994 to highlight and preserve Hispanic culture in Santa Fe and New Mexico. She is a Santa Fe native who left Santa Fe for fifteen years and upon her return was surprised to see "How drastically things had changed and how the culture, and the Spanish language was being lost and in danger of being buried with our parents."

Pacheco felt that the Spanish language was the "glue that keeps the culture together." She stated that by encouraging children to speak Spanish and by educating them about Hispanic customs and festivals, "why we're doing them and why it's being done," the culture would not die out. She also commented that writing and research was important in ensuring the preservation of the Hispanic culture.

Pacheco characterized Santa Fe Hispanic culture as unique because of the blending of Hispanic and Native American roots. With regard to cultural labels, Pacheco commented that *Hispanic* seemed to be the most appropriate label and is the term she uses in her publication. She stated, "Few of us are purely Spanish-American or Mexican-American anymore. I dislike the term 'Chicano,' I'm not that militant. I'm a more mainstream Hispanic."

Tom Chávez

I also interviewed Dr. Tom Chávez (2000), noted Santa Fe author and historian and former director of the Palace of the Governors in Santa Fe. He is now director of the National Hispanic Cultural Center in Albuquerque. He commented that people do not have to be historians to be aware of their Santa Fe Hispanic culture. He said, "The Hispanic heritage of Santa Fe is reflected in the names of the streets, the lay-out of the town, the food we eat, it's kind of obvious." Chávez pointed to the family as the central vehicle for transmitting Hispanic cultural identity in Santa Fe.

Chávez did not believe that the local culture was in danger of being lost. He stated, "If you ask anyone, anywhere in the world to define what their culture is, they would say a couple of things, but after that, they would be at a loss. Cultures are always in transition. For a culture to survive, it changes, and the Hispanic culture has changed throughout history." Chávez elaborated: "The world's shrinking. It's not just us who are being influenced by Coca-Cola or hamburgers anymore. Hamburgers are good and so [they] spread. But we're survivors; we've maintained our culture for 400 years. Let's have a little confidence in the roots our ancestors put down."

Chávez felt that the best way to maintain Santa Fe Hispanic culture was not to fear other cultures or new information and knowledge. He believed that a strong culture would embrace outside influences. He commented, "Look at the Spanish language, everywhere you go it embraced local languages, whether it be Indian or English. That's what strong cultures do. The language will evolve just like the culture. My fear is that we don't try to freeze the culture in a place and time because that will kill it."

Chávez stated that from the very beginning, Santa Fe developed a unique culture. A main reason for this uniqueness, he stated, was the fact that the city was landlocked without a port. The geographic isolation of the region led to a culture that developed with few outside influences. He commented, "We were an island in the wilderness really, but the people here tended to like it that way. They preferred the Mother countries of

Spain and Mexico to send money and supplies but then leave us alone." He explained that this led to unique ways of doing things and seeing the world. He cited the Penitente religious movement as an example.

Rudólfo Anaya

In an article written by David Alire Garcia for *Crosswinds Weekly* in 1999, interviews were conducted with a variety of New Mexico Hispano writers and leaders to determine if the native Hispanic culture in New Mexico was fading. Rudólfo Anaya, popular New Mexican writer, stated in Garcia's article, "Perhaps culture is 'evolving' or 'transforming.' Cultures are organic, they're constantly changing and one of those changes is that we're becoming English speakers and that's all right. Cultures affect each other and change each other" (Garcia, p. 11).

Anaya later commented in the article, "The question is: Can we be a Hispanic, English-speaking culture? That's what we're becoming. My answer is yes, if we retain our soul" (Garcia, p. 11).

Father Jerome Martinez y Alire

Garcia also interviewed Father Jerome Martinez y Alire, former rector at St. Francis Cathedral in Santa Fe. Martinez y Alire commented, "Native Hispanic culture has always been evolving" (p. 8). He also stated, "It [Hispanic culture] was always a culture that was willing to intermarry and learn the very best of each culture" (Garcia, p. 8).

Dr. Edward T. Hall

In an interview I conducted with Dr. Edward T. Hall, founder of the field of intercultural communication and a resident of Santa Fe, on October 25, 1999, he related the following story to illustrate the nature of Santa Fe Hispanic cultural identity. When Hall was once visiting Athens, he met a woman in the Greek Embassy who commented to him, "I'm a German when I'm in Germany, but when I'm in Athens, I'm a Greek." Hall (1999) asked, "How many roles do Santa Fe Hispanics play?" Hall added, "For Santa Fe Hispanics educated and enculturated in an Anglo educational system for several generations, one must look at what remains. What makes a Santa Fe Hispanic different from an Anglo?"

In the final analysis Santa Fe Hispanic culture is shaped by a myriad of influences. Tom Chávez (2000) stated, "The culture isn't dictated by academics, it comes from the people, it comes from the streets."

Santa Fe Culture from a Citizen's Perspective

In addition to interviewing Santa Fe Hispanics who had invested considerable effort in understanding the local Hispanic culture, I conducted personal interviews with a sample of Santa Fe residents in order to gain a better understanding of how Santa Fe Hispanic culture is perceived by the larger Santa Fe population and what identification labels are most widely used and preferred in referring to the Santa Fe Hispanic population.

I gathered data from forty-two Santa Fe Hispanic and twenty-eight non-Hispanic residents of Santa Fe in 1999. Respondents were chosen to represent a diverse range of backgrounds and demographics. Some thirty-seven female Santa Fe residents and thirty-three male residents were selected, representing a wide range of ages, from fifteen to seventy-six. The respondents were employed in a broad range of professions throughout the city including a nurse, secretary, teacher, homemaker, government employee, banker, student, and others. Respondents were selected by visiting various locations in the city in an attempt to represent a wide cross-section of the Santa Fe community.

I approached each of the respondents and asked if I could conduct a brief, five-minute interview with them for a study that I was conducting regarding Hispanic cultural identity in Santa Fe. Most of the respondents agreed to take part in the interview without delay and sat down for an interview immediately. Approximately ten respondents agreed to be interviewed but asked me to return at an alternate time that was more convenient for them. Five people declined to participate and alternate respondents were selected.

I asked the respondents what cultural identification term he/she felt was most appropriate in defining Santa Fe's "Hispanic" population (see Table 2). *Hispanic* was the strong preference in terminology for both Hispanic and non-Hispanic respondents in Santa Fe. *Latino* and *Spanish-American* enjoyed a lesser degree of popularity with both Hispanic and non-Hispanic Santa Feans.

Table 2. Ethnic Identification Preferences of Santa Feans

Identification	Hispanic Number	Percentage	Non-Hispanic Number	Percentage
1. Hispanic	28	67%	17	61%
2. Latino	5	12%	3	11%
3. Spanish-American	5	12%	6	21%
4. Hispano	2	5%	0	0%
5. Chicano	1	2%	0	0%
6. Latin-American	1	2%	0	0%
7. Mexican	0	0%	1	3.5%
8. Don't Know	0	0%	1	3.5%
Totals	42	100%	28	100%

I asked each interviewee to explain his or her choice based on the individual's personal understanding of the term he or she chose. The following question was posed to each interviewee: "What cultural or ethnic label do you feel is most appropriate when referring to Santa Feans who are of Spanish or Mexican descent, and what are your reasons for this preference?" The following are examples of comments I received.

Several Hispanic Santa Feans commented that they used the term *Hispanic* simply because it was the term that seemed to be most universal. Some statements included:

"It's the most common term for [the] Spanish-speaking people of Santa Fe," "Hispanic is the term I've grown up with," "It's how we refer to ourselves," "It's what I've always known," "It's what I was taught," and "It's the term used on all the Federal forms."

Another factor that Hispanic Santa Feans cited for using the term *Hispanic* was that it was more inclusive and encompassing. Some comments included: "It encompasses different groups," "Hispanic is less race-oriented," "It includes [Santa Fe] natives and Mexicans," "It includes the increasing numbers of Mexicans and South Americans in Santa Fe," and "Hispanic brings us all together and gives us more cultural and political clout."

A third reason for choosing the term *Hispanic* was the implication that it suggested a Spanish heritage. One interviewee commented, "It represents people who speak Spanish and have a Spanish background." Other remarks included: "Hispanic emphasizes that my relatives came from Spain," "The label shows that our primary influence is Spanish," and "It defines our Spanish heritage."

Two interviewees stated that they preferred *Hispano* because it was a term that reflected the Spanish language more than did other terms.

Non-Hispanic Santa Feans that I interviewed also preferred the term *Hispanic* most often, for many of the same reasons voiced by Hispanic Santa Feans. The three main reasons for the preference cited by non-Hispanic respondents were the common usage of the term, the inclusiveness of the term, and the identification of Spanish heritage.

Latino proved to be the second-most popular term cited by respondents. The reason cited most often by those choosing *Latino* was that the term was inclusive of all different kinds of Spanish-speaking cultures and backgrounds. The reasoning for choosing *Latino* as a label was similar to the reasons that other respondents had given for choosing the term *Hispanic*. The preference between the two terms appeared to be that the younger respondents (fifteen to thirty years of age) seemed to be more familiar with the term *Latino*. As one subject commented, "Latino is more of the 'new age' modern term." Another respondent said, "I learned to use the term in my high school MEChA club,[2] it seemed to be the term that younger people liked to use."

Spanish-American is also a term commonly used in Santa Fe. The subjects who picked this term voiced a common view that the term emphasized the Spanish origins of the descendants of the explorers and settlers. One Hispanic commented, "I think Spanish-American is most appropriate because many families can trace their lineage back to the period of Spanish exploration hundreds of years ago."

Chicano was a term that was chosen by only one respondent but was mentioned by several people. *Chicano* was not a popular term with the interviewees. Several comments were made by Hispanics and non-Hispanics that the term was "slang" or "too militant" or "radical."

SANTA FE HISPANIC CULTURAL CHARACTERISTICS

I also attempted to explore the qualities or characteristics of Santa Fe Hispanic culture that came to mind for Santa Fe residents that most clearly defined or represented Santa Fe Hispanic culture for them. Table 3 shows the responses from both Hispanic and non-Hispanic respondents. The forty-two Hispanic respondents and twenty-eight non-Hispanic respondents reported several characteristics of Santa Fe Hispanic culture and some offered only one response.

Values and beliefs[3] were often cited as important qualities in defining Santa Fe Hispanic culture. The two most commonly cited values by both Hispanic and non-Hispanic Santa Feans were religion and close family bonds. One Hispanic Santa Fean commented, "We have strong family ties to each other. We're inter-generational. Our families consist of grandparents, children, and our children's children." Another Hispanic stated, "There is a strong bond between Hispanic families you don't see anywhere else." Non-Hispanics also noted the strong family ties in characterizing the culture. Comments included such comments as "The closeness of the extended family," "tight family bonds," and "very family-oriented."

The Catholic religion was often cited as a key Hispanic cultural influence: "Strong, uniquely New Mexican Catholic beliefs, the Santuario is an example," "religious devotion, particularly in the elderly," "deep religious beliefs evident in the architecture, art, and social values."

Other values and beliefs that were mentioned as characterizing Santa Fe Hispanic culture included "cultural pride," "love of the land," "hospitality," and "a sense of community."

Not all comments regarding Santa Fe Hispanic cultural values and beliefs were positive in nature. Respondents mentioned "machismo," "anger and insecurity," "territorial," and "loss of culture" as cultural characteristics as well.

Physical manifestations of culture were often mentioned as being characteristics of Santa Fe Hispanic culture. Food topped the list of responses for both Hispanics and non-Hispanics. Art, music, dance, architecture, clothing, and the Santa Fe Fiesta also were mentioned.

The responses from the interviewees regarding perceived Santa Fe Hispanic cultural characteristics provide insight into the components of cultural identity that Santa Fe Hispanics have of themselves and the cultural identity that non-Hispanic Santa Fe residents have of Santa Fe Hispanics.

Self-defined cultural identity will be compared in a later chapter to the other-defined identity that is projected by tourism interests and by "others" who view Santa Fe and its Hispanic citizens from an "outside" perspective.

Table 3. Reported Characteristics of Santa Fe Hispanic Culture*

Characteristics Cited	Hispanics	Non-Hispanics
1. Religion	13	8
2. Food	11	7
3. Close family bonds	9	13
4. Spanish language	6	3
5. Music	5	2
6. Art	5	5
7. The Fiesta	4	3
8. Traditions	3	2
9. Dance	2	0
10. Values	2	2
11. Drama	2	0
12. Hospitality	2	0
13. Loss of culture	2	0
14. Architecture	2	3
15. Clothing	1	2
16. Machismo	1	1
17. Sense of community	1	0
18. Respect for land	1	0
19. Unity	1	0
20. Pride	0	1
21. Concept of time	0	1
22. Love of earth	0	1
23. Importance of car	0	1
24. Holidays	0	1
25. Anger	0	1
26. Territorial	0	1
Total number of responses	72	58

*Note: The forty-two Hispanic and twenty-eight non-Hispanic respondents could each provide more than one response.

Conclusions

The cultural self-identity of Santa Fe Hispanics is influenced by a combination of historical and modern events and perceptions. Many attitudes that Santa Fe Hispanics have about their culture are self-defined and are communicated through traditional channels such as family and religion. The arts also play an important role in communicating cultural self-identity. Material manifestations of culture such as food, clothing, language, and architecture were also cited in personal interviews conducted with Santa Fe Hispanos.

Non-Hispanic Santa Fe respondents' ideas regarding Hispanic cultural characteristics were notably similar to responses by Santa Fe Hispanic respondents.

A common theme that emerged in interviews with Hispanic cultural leaders and historians was that Santa Fe Hispanic culture was constantly in a state of transformation and was being redefined. This process was cited as being not an object of concern, but rather a quality of a healthy culture.

The recent influx of Spanish-speaking immigrants from Mexico and Central America have also added a new flavor to the Santa Fe Hispanic community. Along with the benefits of new cultural influences have come increased tensions as the more recent inhabitants of Santa Fe compete with natives for scarce jobs and resources. This divide in the Hispanic community is apparent when one overhears local Hispanics referring to Mexicans as "*mojados*," the Spanish translation for "wetbacks."

Just as cultural identity has changed over time, so have the preferences of Santa Fe Hispanos regarding the ethnic label preferences they prefer. The label *Hispanic* was the preference of most of the respondents interviewed in the present study. Historically, other terms such as *Spanish American* or *Chicano* have enjoyed popularity, but are preferred less often presently.

The exploration of Hispanic cultural identity in Santa Fe yielded a complex picture of how it is defined and understood. Although pinpointing its characteristics can be elusive, there was general agreement that its preservation was important. The concept that culture and cultural identity are not static but rather in a state of constant transformation was also emphasized. The ability of a culture to expand and change but also to retain its unique and defining characteristics appear to be important ingredients in maintaining a healthy, vigorous culture. Just as cultural labels for Hispanics have shifted over the years as a result of in-group and out-group influences, so do the overall perceptions of culture and cultural identity.

CHAPTER FOUR

Fiesta de Santa Fe

As the primary Hispanic cultural festival in Santa Fe, the Fiesta de Santa Fe plays a major role in reflecting and transmitting Hispanic cultural identity.

HISTORICAL BACKGROUND

The origins of the Fiesta de Santa Fe (hereafter also referred to as the "Fiesta") can be traced to 1712. The Fiesta has a complex history that reflects many transformations since its origin. The character of the Fiesta has been shaped by the Santa Fe Hispanic community and by outside influences, making it both a self-defined and other-defined ritual. To more fully explore the development and character of the Fiesta, it is necessary to begin by reviewing the historical background of the Fiesta de Santa Fe.

La Conquistadora

The first event in a series of occurrences that would eventually materialize into the Fiesta de Santa Fe occurred in 1625. While in Mexico City, Fray Alonso de Benavides, a Franciscan priest, came across a wooden statue that he believed would provide inspiration to the hard-pressed settlers of the northern frontier. The twenty-eight-inch tall statue depicted a Marian figure carved in willow wood that was of fine craftsmanship (see Figure 8). He purchased the statue and when he and eleven other Franciscans traveled to Santa Fe in 1625, the statue accompanied them (Chávez, 1985). The statue resided in the Santa Fe parroquia (parish) where she acted as an important religious symbol for Spanish pioneers. Sometime between 1625 and 1655, a Rosary confraternity was founded around the statue's presence and she was given the name of "Nuestra Señora del Rosario" because of her affiliation to the confraternity. In addition to this title, she was given the name of "La Conquistadora" to honor the original Spanish pioneers to New Mexico (Chávez, 1985).

Thomas E. Chávez (1985) pointed out that the statue became known as "Nuestra Señora de la Conquistadora" before the Indian Revolt of 1680, when there was no formal acknowledgment of a formal conquest in New Mexico. He explained that a formal definition of "*conquistar*," or to conquer, is to win one's affections, and this was the intended meaning of La Conquistadora's name.

La Conquistadora sat in Santa Fe as a symbol of Spanish religious devotion until 1680, when the Pueblo Revolt drove the Spaniards from Santa Fe to El Paso del Norte (today's El Paso). La Conquistadora, who was rescued from a fire during the Revolt, retreated with the Spaniards and did not return to Santa Fe until thirteen years later, when she accompanied Don Diego de Vargas in the Spanish reconquest. It is this connection between La Conquistadora and De Vargas that provides the basis for the Fiesta de Santa Fe celebration.

DE VARGAS AND THE SANTA FE FIESTA

The *entradas* (entries) into Santa Fe led by De Vargas in 1692 and 1693 were the basis for the formation of the Santa Fe Fiesta celebration. The reconquest of Santa Fe made De Vargas a revered figure in his time.

In 1712, eight years following De Vargas's death, Don Juan Paez Hurtado, who had served as De Vargas's lieutenant governor, drafted a resolution proclaiming that an annual fiesta would commemorate the reconquest and De Vargas's memory. The year 1712 is formally cited as the historical beginning of the Fiesta de Santa Fe (Grimes, 1976).

De Vargas and La Conquistadora are forever entwined in Fiesta lore. De Vargas's religious devotion was displayed by the banners of the Marian figure he carried during his entradas into Santa Fe in 1692 and 1693. Pedro Ribera-Ortega, Santa Fe historian and author, wrote that De Vargas petitioned La Conquistadora that if she would assist him in the reconquest of New Mexico he would promise to honor her annually. He also vowed to establish a throne of honor for her in New Mexico. After the reconquest in 1693, De Vargas had La Conquistadora enshrined in a chapel in the Casa Reales, while a new church was built to fulfill his promise. The new chapel was completed in 1714.

Since the Fiesta proclamation of 1712, La Conquistadora and Don Diego de Vargas have remained the two central figures in the Santa Fe celebration.

Figure 8.
La Conquistadora, 1948.
Photo by Robert H. Martin.
La Conquistadora as she
appeared in the Rosario
Chapel during the Santa Fe
Fiesta of 1948. Courtesy
the Museum of New
Mexico, #41984.

Fiesta Evolution

First celebrations honoring La Conquistadora and Don Diego de Vargas's memory after the 1712 proclamation were not well documented during the 1700s and for most of the 1800s. Wilson (1997) stated that it appears the event lapsed for a time in the mid-1700s. The celebration was revived in 1770 and has been regularly observed since then.

During the early years of the Fiesta, the event was mainly religious in nature. The "Corpus Christi" Catholic celebration and the Conquistadora processions were the primary points of focus. Anthropologist Ronald Grimes (1976) observed that the Corpus Christi procession and the La Conquistadora processions performed in Santa Fe were very similar. He noted that they were ordered in much the same way, involving "sacred displays, worship and praise, and the reception of divine grace and favor" (p. 58).

The religious processions through Santa Fe were formally connected with Don Diego de Vargas's reconquest when a chapel named "Rosario" was built in 1807 on the spot where La Conquistadora was believed to have sat during De Vargas's entry into Santa Fe. The Rosario Chapel has been the important landmark in the Conquistadora processions from the time of its construction.

The Fiesta continued as a religious festival reflecting local devotion during the Spanish and Mexican rule in Santa Fe. As the nature of Santa Fe began to change after New Mexico became a U.S. territory in 1850, and as Anglo presence and influence increased, the Santa Fe Fiesta was also gradually transformed.

American immigrants from the eastern United States countered the indigenous Fiesta celebration with their own Fourth of July celebration. In 1883, the two events merged into what would become the prototype for future Fiesta events. The catalyst for the Fiesta transformation was the 1883 Tertio-Millennial Exposition held in Santa Fe, which commemorated the 333-year anniversary of the founding of the city. A fair amount of historical revisionism was necessary to make this claim, as 1550 was a date of no particular significance to Santa Fe. The true purpose of the 1883 exposition was to promote local businesses and natural resources to investors and to enhance tourism (Wilson, 1997). The three-day exposition featured displays by local businessmen and farmers, horse races, parades, and music. The first day's theme was Indian culture, the second day featured Spanish history with a reenactment of Don Diego de Vargas's entrada, and the final day focused on Anglo-American culture (Chávez, 1985). From this point forward, the Fiesta celebration ceased to be a purely Hispanic religious festival. The Fiesta became a more civic celebration.

As New Mexico neared imminent statehood status in 1911, the Fiesta/Fourth of July celebration continued to feature the reenactment of the entrada as a major part of the festivities. George Washington Armijo, a former Rough Rider with Teddy Roosevelt during the Spanish-American War, portrayed Don Diego de Vargas. In an interesting example of cultural tolerance, both the Mexican and U.S. national anthems were played. In 1912, the celebration flourished, feeding off the enthusiasm of newly acquired statehood. Participation in the planning and execution of the

Fiesta came from several sectors of the community, including the Santa Fe Chamber of Commerce, the Alianza Hispano-Americana, and the Museum of New Mexico.

Interestingly, in spite of the popularity and success of the celebrations in 1911 and 1912, the Fiesta festivities were dropped for the next six years, not to be revived until 1919. Several circumstances led to this lull in activity. The Museum of New Mexico's preoccupation with the San Diego Exposition and the national focus on World War 1 were major factors (Wilson, 1997).

The revived Fiesta celebration of 1919 was a turning point for the festival. The Fiesta was moved from its Fourth of July date to September. The Museum of New Mexico and School of American Research, made up of eastern-educated Anglos, organized the event. The Fiesta focused on the three dominant cultures of Santa Fe with a day devoted to each. Although the Fiesta was incorporated into the Museum of New Mexico's cultural revival effort, Hispanic participation dropped sharply in contrast to past Fiesta celebrations. Even though George Washington Armijo agreed to play the role of Don Diego de Vargas as in the past, Anglo men portrayed most of his Cuadrilla (troops).

Wilson (1997) speculated that the decline in Hispanic participation might have been in part the result of the commercialization of the Fiesta. In a sense, the Fiesta, which had always been a symbol of Hispanic religious and cultural identity, was being appropriated by Anglo culture and redefined by institutions like the Museum of New Mexico.

The Hispanic population of Santa Fe was joined by the new art colony (which was developing in Santa Fe) in its displeasure with the change in the nature of the Fiesta. The Museum of New Mexico, in an attempt to make the Fiesta financially self-sustaining, fenced off certain Fiesta activities and charged admission. These actions had the consequence of pricing out many local people. In response, members of the art community developed a series of alternate activities in the 1920s. The program of free Fiesta events was called "Pasatiempo." These new Fiesta activities included the Hysterical Parade that emphasized fun and exaggerated dress and decoration. There was community singing and dancing in the streets, a children's animal parade, and the infamous "Zozobra" presented by Will Shuster and E. Dana Johnson in 1926 (Wilson, 1997).

Many of the Pasatiempo events came to be permanent, endearing parts of future Fiesta celebrations. In particular, Zozobra has become a prominent figure of the Fiesta.

Artist Will Shuster developed Zozobra in 1924 when he built a puppet based on an effigy of a Judas figure that he saw burned in a ritual in Mexico. During the Fiesta of 1924 he burned his effigy in his backyard for a circle of his friends. The following year, with the assistance of Johnson, editor of *The New Mexican* newspaper, he increased the puppet's size to eighteen feet and gave him the name "Zozobra," which roughly translates as the "gloomy" or "anguished" one in Spanish. In 1926 the first public burning took place, and a Fiesta tradition was born (Chávez, 1985).

The Zozobra burning that occurs each year traditionally signifies the beginning of the Fiesta. The burning symbolizes the discarding of despair and the bad luck of the past year so that Fiesta participants can begin celebrations with a new sense of optimism. In a sense, the paganlike ritual is not unlike a city-wide catharsis (see Figure 9).

The 1920s also saw a renewed emphasis on the religious aspects of the Fiesta. Hispanic participation increased and this renewed interest spurred a revitalized Catholic orientation. The 1920 Fiesta was highlighted by the dedication of the "Cross of the Martyrs." This monument was dedicated to the twenty-one Franciscan friars who were killed during the 1680 Pueblo Revolt. Five years later, in 1925, the candlelight procession to the cross was initiated and has since become a standard Fiesta activity (Wilson, 1997).

During 1927 another important component was added to the evolving Fiesta. The Pasatiempo activities came to include a Fiesta queen to complement the De Vargas role. The Fiesta queen was primarily a Hispanic invention, symbolizing on some levels the devotion to the figure of La Conquistadora and the Virgin Mary. Fiesta masses, the annual knighting of Don Diego de Vargas, and the coronation of the Fiesta queen by the archbishop of Santa Fe in subsequent years reinforced the religious aspects of the Fiesta.

The Fiesta of the Museum of New Mexico and the rival Pasatiempo activities were eventually merged with Hispanic religious activities to form the expanded Fiesta that resembles the modern-day celebration.

In the late 1920s, the Fiesta began to drop its tricultural emphasis and was viewed as a primarily Hispanic cultural festival. As time passed, the

Figure 9. Zozobra, 1954.
Zozobra awaiting his burning
during the 1954 Fiesta de Santa
Fe. Photo by Henry Dendahl,
Courtesy the Museum of New
Mexico, #57753.

local Hispanic community has taken increasing ownership of the Fiesta.
Simultaneously, as the Fiesta has evolved in recent years, the various
influences that have shaped the Fiesta have blended to produce a celebration that borrows from its multicultural past.

Zozobra and the Hysterical/Historical Parade, the products of past
Anglo influence, exist next to traditional Hispanic ceremonies such as the
La Conquistadora processions and the candlelight procession to the Cross
of the Martyrs.

FIESTA CONTROVERSY

The Fiesta de Santa Fe has not been without its controversy over the years.
In 1964 the archdiocese of Santa Fe withdrew its support from the Fiesta
because of its perception that the Fiesta had become too commercialized

and was losing its religious focus. The archdiocese of Santa Fe reluctantly agreed to reinstate its support in 1966 after receiving assurances from the Fiesta Council that future celebrations would place more emphasis on religious aspects (Grimes, 1976).

The Fiesta celebration continued to grow in the 1960s and began to attract large numbers of visitors from outside of Santa Fe who knew little about the history and meaning of the Fiesta. The celebration was thus threatened with the loss of its ethnic and religious character. The definitive event that prompted Fiesta officials to shift the date of Fiesta activities away from the Labor Day holiday was the civil disturbance during the 1971 Fiesta, in which widespread vandalism and confrontations with Santa Fe police occurred. About one hundred National Guard reserves were called in to restore order on the Plaza. This incident has since been referred to by locals as the "Fiesta Riots" and led to a movement to make the Fiesta smaller and more local. Many long-time Fiesta participants lost enthusiasm following the 1971 incident, and the Fiesta has held the stigma of danger for them ever since. A comment often made by locals is that the best time to leave Santa Fe is during the Fiesta. In past years there have been rumors that outside groups such as outlaw bikers, Los Angeles gang members, or Nazi skinheads were coming to Santa Fe to cause trouble during the Fiesta (Terrell, 1993). In 1972, in an attempt to make the Fiesta more manageable, the Fiesta dates were changed to avoid coinciding with the Labor Day weekend.

Another incident, which shook the foundations of the Santa Fe Fiesta, took place in 1973. On March 19, 1973, La Conquistadora was stolen. If there was any doubt about the continuing importance of the statue to city residents, this incident dispelled it. The church, local media, and public officials raised their voices in concern and outrage over the incident, and various local groups raised reward money. On March 25, 1973, a "day of mourning" was declared by the mayor of Santa Fe and bells tolled in the city. Church leaders asked citizens to pray for La Conquistadora's return (Grimes, 1976). On April 15, 1973, La Conquistadora was found after a massive search led by state and city police. Two local teenage boys were arrested and named as the culprits after their failed attempt at extorting a ransom of $150,000. The return of the statue was marked by a solemn procession led by city officials. The mayor called the return of La Conquistadora "a most memorable day in the history of Santa Fe" (Grimes, 1976).

A 1992 video documentary about the Santa Fe Fiesta, *Gathering Up Again: Fiesta in Santa Fe*, by Jeanette DeBouzek and Diane Reyna examined the celebration with a critical eye. It explored the aspects of the Fiesta that dealt with the portrayal of the reconquest as a "bloodless" event and how the Fiesta failed to reflect the Pueblo Indian perspective.

The release of the video generated debate and comments from a variety of Hispanic and Pueblo Indian leaders. Herman Agoyo, executive director of the Eight Northern Indian Pueblos Council, stated that the Fiesta "still smacked of oppression" and "should be done away with" (Easthouse, 1993). Joseph Suina, a Cochiti Pueblo Indian professor from the University of New Mexico, characterized the Fiesta as "a celebration that takes place at the expense of other people; it's not a celebration, it's a put-down" (Easthouse, 1993). Santa Fe Hispanic historian and writer Orlando Romero countered that the video portrayed a historically inaccurate version of the Fiesta and that the modern Fiesta is more of a "time to celebrate and shed the wounds that we have caused each other." Likewise, Tom Chávez, a Santa Fe historian, stated that much of the criticism of the Fiesta was based on misunderstanding and the tendency to portray Hispanics in the mold of the "Black Legend," which perpetuates negative connotations of Spanish descendants.

Pressure for changes in the Fiesta had been building for years as criticism from Pueblo leaders and others grew. In 1992 Archbishop Robert Sanchez gave La Conquistadora an additional name, "Nuestra Señora de la Paz," or "Our Lady of Peace." A "Mass of Reconciliation" was added to Fiesta events and a greater effort was made to present Indians and Spaniards as equals. Fiesta Council President Rick Berardinelli stated that these changes were made to extend "a hand of friendship" to the Pueblos. He commented, "We've been concentrating a great deal on the healing of our respective cultures" (Duke, 1992).

The documentary was not the first incident to expose ruffled relations between Pueblo Indians and Fiesta organizers. In 1977, Fiesta Council President Gilbert Valdez sent a letter to the Museum of New Mexico director, George Ewing, stating his desire to remove Indian vendors from

Table 4. Fiesta de Santa Fe Timeline

DATE	EVENT
1625	Fray Alonzo de Benavides, a Franciscan priest, brings the wooden statue of La Conquistadora to Santa Fe.
1680	During the Pueblo Revolt, La Conquistadora is rescued and taken to El Paso del Norte by the fleeing Spaniards.
1692–1693	Don Diego de Vargas leads the reconquest of Santa Fe after petitioning La Conquistadora for assistance and promising to honor her if he was successful.
1693	La Conquistadora is enshrined in a chapel in the Casa Reales, while a church in her honor is built.
1712	Eight years following Don Diego de Vargas's death, Don Paez Hurtado drafts a resolution proclaiming the reconquest of Santa Fe and De Vargas's memory would be commemorated by an annual Fiesta. The year 1712 is the formally cited beginning of the Santa Fe Fiesta.
1726–1769	The Fiesta celebration is observed inconsistently with lapses in the mid-1700s.
1770	The Confraternity of La Conquistadora revives the Fiesta celebration.
1807	Rosario Chapel is built and the first Fiesta procession takes place.
1883	The Fiesta and Fourth of July celebrations are merged during the Tertio-Millennial Exposition. The Fiesta becomes a more civic celebration.
1913–1918	The Fiesta lapses due to World War I and preoccupation with the San Diego Exposition in 1915.

the Plaza area during the Fiesta. This request was pointed to by Indian leaders as proof that Indians were not welcome during the Fiesta and an Indian boycott was threatened. After a retraction from Valdez and a personal plea from Mayor Sam Pick, the boycott was diverted. However, this incident was an example of the Pueblo Indians' sensitivity to the Fiesta celebration.

In recent years, the main concerns surrounding the Fiesta centered on the question of violence. Reflecting modern society, fear of gang-related violence has been of particular concern. On July 3, 1993, Francisco "Pancho" Ortega was shot by Santa Fe Police.[1] There were rumors of possible organized violence during the Fiesta to protest his death. The anticipated violence did not materialize. However, many residents avoided the Fiesta that year as a precaution. In 1997, a gang-related murder took place

DATE	EVENT
1919	The Fiesta is revived under the influence and direction of the Museum of New Mexico.
1926	The first public burning of Zozobra takes place.
1927	The first Fiesta queen is introduced into the Fiesta celebration.
1930–1960	The Fiesta becomes established as a community civic celebration.
1964	The archdiocese of Santa Fe withdraws from the Fiesta, citing overcommercialization.
1971	One hundred National Guard troops are called in to restore order during the Fiesta after civil disturbances and vandalism occurs.
1972	The Fiesta celebration is moved from Labor Day weekend to discourage the influx of outsiders and to keep the Fiesta more manageable.
1973	On March 19, La Conquistadora is stolen; it is recovered on April 15. Two local teenage boys unsuccessfully attempt to extort ransom for her return.
1992	The video documentary *Gathering Up Again: Fiesta in Santa Fe* stirs controversy as it incites debate about the nature of the Fiesta celebration as a festival celebrating the oppression of the Pueblo Indians.
1993	Police shooting of Francisco "Pancho" Ortega sparks fears of rioting during the Fiesta, but no violence materializes.
1997	A gang-related shooting takes place on the Santa Fe Plaza following the burning of Zozobra. This murder leads to a decision to move the burning from Friday night to Thursday night during future Fiesta celebrations.

on the Plaza shortly after the burning of Zozobra. This murder led to the decision to move the Zozobra burning from a Friday night, which was traditionally followed by music and dancing on the Plaza, to Thursday night followed by no festivities. The rationale for this change was a "safer Fiesta."

The Cultural Nature of the Fiesta

As a remote northern outpost, the isolation that Santa Fe experienced during its formative years from the Spanish and Mexican seats of power led to the development of its unique Hispanic culture. While certainly influenced by the Spanish and Mexican cultures, Santa Fe created a culture characteristically its own. The local Hispanic culture has also been transformed and influenced by its contact with the Pueblo Indian and

American Anglo cultures. These circumstances and varied other influences have led to a cultural identity that is a complex mixture of tradition and invention. In many ways, the Santa Fe Fiesta is an appropriate metaphor for Santa Fe Hispanic cultural identity as a whole.

In the same way that communication scholars Porter and Samovar (1997) described culture as dynamic and subject to invention and diffusion, the Santa Fe Fiesta has continued to change over time. Originally, the Fiesta was a festival that was mainly religious in nature, honoring the memory of Don Diego de Vargas and the reconquest of Santa Fe.

As the culture of Santa Fe was transformed after the American occupation, the Fiesta inevitably mirrored this change. The Tertio-Millennial Exposition in 1883 marked a turning point in the Fiesta as it began to shift away from an exclusively Hispanic cultural and religious celebration to a more commercialized event with an increasing Anglo-American influence. This shift continued into the 1900s as New Mexico neared statehood. The Fiesta celebrations of 1911 and 1912 combined the Fiesta with Fourth of July festivities to produce a hybrid celebration.

The period from 1919 through the early 1920s saw the Fiesta heavily influenced by the Museum of New Mexico and its primarily Anglo staff. The Museum's presence led to a backlash from a coalition of "counter-culture" Anglo artists and Hispanic natives who disliked the commercialization of the Fiesta that they perceived to be taking place. In response, a renewed Hispanic emphasis on maintaining the religious focus of the Fiesta occurred, while art colony activists added community events such as Zozobra and Pasatiempo activities.

Over the years from the 1930s through the present, the nature of the Fiesta has been a barometer reflecting, as well as influencing, the culture of Santa Feans. The constant battle between tradition and commercialism that characterized the city as a whole has been, and continues to be, a main concern in relation to the Fiesta.

THE SANTA FE FIESTA AS A VEHICLE FOR
SANTA FE HISPANIC CULTURAL IDENTITY

Intercultural communication authors Lustig and Koester (1999) stated that cultural identity is transmitted via "traditions, heritage, language, religion, ancestry, aesthetics, thinking patterns, and social structures" (p. 138). The Santa Fe Fiesta provides a vehicle for the transfer of each of these elements, to a certain degree, for Santa Fe Hispanics. These means of conveying cultural identity are embedded in the Fiesta in the various events that take place during the annual celebration. For example, the major masses that are held during Fiesta (De Vargas mass, Pontifical mass, and Thanksgiving mass) not only transmit religious cultural identification, but also convey information regarding other aspects of cultural identity. The traditional dress of the Fiesta royalty, the mariachi music, the ceremony, and the rituals performed in conjunction with the masses (i.e., the blessing of De Vargas and the Fiesta queen by the archbishop) touch upon tradition, heritage, aesthetics, and other vehicles of cultural identity.

In many ways, the Fiesta is a celebration of Santa Fe Hispanic culture. Arts and crafts booths displaying the work of Hispanic artists line the Plaza; food booths are in abundance, selling traditional cuisine; the Plaza bandstand features Hispanic musicians and dancers; and De Vargas, the Fiesta queen, and their entourage visit locations throughout the city in conjunction with the Fiesta.

The Santa Fe Hispanic population may face the prospect of soaring housing costs, a stagnant job market, and an inadequate public school system, but at least for Fiesta weekend, Hispanic culture is dominant in Santa Fe.

1999 Fiesta Interviews

I conducted a series of personal interviews with key participants in the 1999 Fiesta in order to gather insight concerning the importance of the Santa Fe Fiesta in promoting Hispanic cultural identity. The following are summaries from those interviews.

Elizabeth Rosa Lovato

Elizabeth Rosa Lovato (1999), the 1999 *La Reina* (Fiesta queen), saw the Fiesta as an opportunity for Santa Fe Hispanics to understand what it means to be Hispanic and "to be proud of our culture and our past." Her favorite part of the role as the Fiesta queen was the visitations she made to schools and to nursing homes. She said, "That's what it's all about. [The] Fiesta spreads cultural pride." Lovato felt it was especially important to involve younger

Santa Fe Hispanics in the Fiesta. She felt the Hispanic culture in Santa Fe was not taught or supported very well outside of the Fiesta. She stated that the local culture was in danger of being lost but the situation was not hopeless. She felt that the visitations the Fiesta court made to Santa Fe schools were important. "It inspires kids; it's their only shot of culture." She added, "[The] Fiesta is not a celebration of conquest to me; it's a celebration of culture."

Lovato saw the Fiesta as important in establishing cultural identity for Santa Fe Hispanics. As she explained, "It's why we're here! If it weren't for [the] Fiesta, I wouldn't have the feeling I have for my culture." She saw herself as a role model for Hispanic girls. "They need to know who they are and where they came from."

Lovato felt the Fiesta reflected the most important parts of Hispanic culture, which were religious faith, family, song, dance, and music. She stated that the religious aspect was the most important part of the Fiesta. She said, "The Fiesta is based on our religion and our faith." She felt the Fiesta queen's role was to represent the characteristics of La Conquistadora. In fact, the central meaning of the Fiesta for her was the celebration of La Conquistadora. She voiced concern that younger Santa Fe Hispanics did not understand the religious aspects of the Fiesta. She noted that most of the people attending the *Novena* masses were from older generations. She added, "When you are young, it's just a big party, but when you know what it's about, you respect it."

Lovato also commented that outside of the religious aspects, the Fiesta had become too commercialized. She said, "I don't know if it can become less commercial, it takes a lot of money to run the Fiesta. If you keep the real part in your heart, the commercial part can be tolerated."

An article in the September 7, 1999, edition of *The New Mexican* newspaper supported Lovato's view. In 1999 there were about 140 people on the Fiesta Council[2] compared to 40 members in 1972. The budget for the Fiesta in 1972 was $40,000, compared to the 1999 budget of $270,000 (Davila, 1999, September 7).

Tommy Trujillo

Tommy Trujillo (1999) portrayed Don Diego de Vargas during the 1999 Fiesta. He concurred with Elizabeth Lovato about the meaning of the

Fiesta. He said, "The center of [the] Fiesta is how we pay homage to La Conquistadora. It's like asking, what's the most important thing about Christmas? You can say family, gifts, good food, but it's the birth of Jesus Christ. The same thing with the Fiesta. It's our homage to La Conquistadora, the promise we'll honor her every year. It can become hanging out with your buddies, going to La Fonda, you know, having a blast, and that's good, as long as you keep in mind what's the focus of the Fiesta. Religion is the main focus."

Trujillo stated, "I think if you're a native, you should be part of [the] Fiesta. There are people who live here their whole life, they have no clue." He added, "Taking classes for ten years wouldn't give me as much knowledge of my culture. It was an educational experience. It's amazing!"

Trujillo, a high school business teacher by profession, also felt it was vital to reach out to Santa Fe's Hispanic youth. "Kids need to be educated. If they think the Fiesta is all about eating Navajo tacos and watching Zozobra, that's sad." However, he stated that Zozobra could be used to inspire the youth to learn about their culture. "I think the best way to reach the youth is to create excitement. If you say, 'This is important,' they won't listen to you, but if you create an exciting environment, use that as a tool to increase their understanding of the culture. Use the excitement, like Zozobra as a tool to get the people downtown" (see Figure 10).

Roger Martinez

Roger Martinez (1999), an active Fiesta participant for many years, characterized Fiesta as a "big community celebration of religion and culture." He admitted that many Santa Feans do not understand the meaning of the Fiesta. He stated, "It's not just a big party, the religious and historical aspects should be focused on." He perceived that the older Santa Feans understood the Fiesta more than do the youth. He believed the elderly, in particular, focused more on the religious aspects.

Pedro Ribera-Ortega

Pedro Ribera-Ortega, who passed away in January of 2003, was a Santa Fe author and historian involved in the Santa Fe Fiesta for sixty-six years, since he was five years old. He served as a member of the Fiesta Council, the Caballeros de Vargas, and La Cofradía de La Conquistadora, and was a historical consultant to the Fiesta. In an interview I had with him in 1999, Ribera-Ortega said, "The Fiesta is nothing more than saying, thank you Lord God to our Blessed Mother for bringing us home from exile." He stated, "To me the Fiesta is comprised of two parts; a very religious thanksgiving which takes place in June and consists of novenas and processions, and then in September, the reading of the Fiesta decree."

Casual observers of the Fiesta often overlook the annual novenas and processions that Ribera-Ortega referred to that take place in June and early July. However, they are of considerable importance to Fiesta participants like Ribera-Ortega because of their religious significance. These ceremonies are initiated by the "Corpus Christi" celebration, which emphasizes Catholic worship and reverence. The following week, La Conquistadora processions take place in the city marking the beginning of Santa Fe Fiesta activities for those who focus on the religious aspects.

Ribera-Ortega said the Fiesta's most important events were the mass of Thanksgiving, held before the procession to the Cross of the Martyrs, and the entrada. He stated, "If anyone really wanted to know what the Fiesta was all about, all they would have to do was read the Fiesta decree written by Hurtado in 1712." Ribera-Ortega said, "The decree is the equivalent to Santa Feans of the Declaration of Independence." He said the decree should be read by teachers in the Santa Fe schools before every Fiesta so that students would know what the Fiesta is all about. He called the decree the "heart and soul" of the Fiesta and without it, he said, the Fiesta "means nothing."

The decree or proclamation referred to by Ribera-Ortega was written by Juan Paez Hurtado and signed by the governor in 1712. It established the annual Fiesta celebration in Santa Fe and referred to the Fiesta as having the purpose of "recalling how this villa had been recognized on the fourteenth day of September of the past year sixteen hundred and ninety two by the General Don Diego de Vargas, and that in twenty years no fiesta had been observed, as this villa should have, in honor of the Salutary Cross of Our Redemption, and so that in the future the said fourteenth day be celebrated with Vespers, Mass, Sermon, and Procession through the Main Plaza."

The Symbolic Nature of the Fiesta

Anthropologist Ronald L. Grimes (1976) examined the symbolism contained in the Santa Fe Fiesta in his book *Symbol and Conquest: Public Ritual and Drama in Santa Fe*. Grimes defined the Fiesta as a "variety of performances including pageants and melodramas which condense Santa Fe's history into symbolic actions" (p. 16). The central question he asks in his book relates to the nature of the Santa Fe Fiesta: Is the Fiesta mainly civic, religious, or ethnic in character?

Grimes (1976) concurred with many local Hispanics in his assessment that the Fiesta has lost much of its traditional focus in recent years. He wrote that the influx of new residents and tourists has led to the perception that the Fiesta is in danger of losing its "local-regional character" and religious underpinnings. He commented that in his observations, sometimes purist views are expressed that the Fiesta should be exclusively religious, ethnic, or civic in nature. However, he stated that these views are not shared by the majority of the Fiesta participants: "Most see no conflict between worshipping and drinking a moderate amount of beer or between the Archbishop and Fiesta queen" (p. 95).

In 1965 the goals that characterize the Fiesta were drafted by the president of the Caballeros De Vargas:

1. To render Almighty God grateful thanksgiving for the reconquests of 1692 and 1693.

2. To promote inherent pride in Santa Fe's dramatic past.

3. To promote gaiety and neighborliness of a true community celebration.

4. To pass on such a venerable tradition to future generations.

(Grimes, 1976, p. 97)

The Santa Fe Fiesta Council described the Fiesta as a community celebration open to all regardless of cultural background or religious affiliation. However, Grimes noted that the Fiesta is hardly nondenominational. Although there are not requirements that state that the Fiesta participants, such as the De Vargas staff or the queen's court, be Roman Catholic, it is expected that they will participate in a variety of Catholic

Figure 10. 1999 De Vargas and Fiesta Queen. Tommy Trujillo, 1999 Santa Fe Fiesta Don Diego De Vargas, and Elizabeth Rosa Lovato, 1999 Fiesta Queen posing with La Conquistadora. Photo by Joe E. Lovato „ 1999.

masses and processions. As a result, there have been few non-Catholic participants or non-Hispanics in these roles over the years. The roles of De Vargas and the Fiesta queen are limited to those of Spanish surname and descent, and they must be bilingual in Spanish and English.

Several groups work on different aspects of the Fiesta to create the finished product that the public sees. The Santa Fe Fiesta Council oversees the entire Fiesta but it depends heavily on other groups. The Caballeros De Vargas is a civic/religious men's group that actively participates in the Fiesta and is most visible during the annual entrada pageant where members portray members of De Vargas's staff in a reenactment of the 1692 entrance of De Vargas into Santa Fe. The Cofradía de La Conquistadora cares for the statue of La Conquistadora and the associated chapels, and runs the novenas and processions associated with La Conquistadora. The Catholic Church also plays a vital role by holding masses supporting Fiesta activities. The Santa Fe Kiwanis Club oversees the construction and burning of Zozobra, and various other groups participate in organizing and conducting events associated with the Fiesta celebrations.

Anglo participation tends to be concentrated in non-Catholic activities such as the Zozobra burning, the Children's Pet Parade, and the Hysterical/Historical Parade. Indian participants are usually scarce, appearing as Fiesta entertainers/dancers on the Plaza bandstand, occasionally representing historical figures during the entrada reenactment, or playing roles in the De Vargas Cuadrilla or the Fiesta queen's court as Indian princesses.

Grimes (1976) saw the Fiesta as a manifestation of a considerable amount of Hispanic-Catholic power in Santa Fe. He argued that it takes a substantial amount of cultural power to define a mainly Hispanic-Catholic festival as a "civic" celebration. He viewed the Fiesta queen as symbolizing civic, cooperative power; the statue of La Conquistadora symbolizing the power of conversion; and De Vargas being a symbol for the power of conquest.

THE 1999 FIESTA

The Fiesta of 1999 reflected attitudes related to Santa Fe Hispanic cultural identity and how Santa Fe history was perceived. The 1999 Fiesta's schedule of events began with the annual historical lecture on Saturday, August 14. Doug Peterson, a Santa Fe Community College professor and a historical guide at El Rancho de Las Golondrinas gave the lecture at Rosario Chapel. The theme of the lecture was life in "The De Vargas Period," focusing on the Pueblo Revolt, the subsequent Spanish retreat in 1680, and the return led by De Vargas in 1692. The lecture was attended by the honorary Don Diego de Vargas, Tommy Trujillo, and fifteen members of his Cuadrilla; the 1999 Fiesta queen, Elizabeth Rosa Lovato, and a *Princesa*; various members of the Fiesta Council; and interested local citizens.

The lecture, which lasted about one hour, was an account of the general history of Santa Fe during the period from 1680 to 1692 and addressed the trials and tribulations of the Spaniards during this period. Peterson's account of the reconquest made little mention of the 1693 battle between De Vargas and the Pueblo Indians occupying Santa Fe or the casualties and executions that followed the 1693 reconquest.

ZOZOBRA

The first event that many Santa Feans have associated with the beginning of the Fiesta is the annual burning of Zozobra. The burning took place on

Thursday, September 9, at about 9:00 P.M., in Fort Marcy Park. About thirty thousand people witnessed the event. The burning was a peaceful, family event in which security was insured by a beefed-up police force of 170 officers (Davila, 1999, September 7).

The 1999 Zozobra was approximately fifty feet tall with orange and yellow hair, green eyes, red lips, and a black belt. His cremation took less than five minutes as he swayed his arms, turned his head from side to side, and groaned in misery. Many in the crowd yelled, "Burn!" as the symbol of bad luck and sorrow disintegrated into ashes.

Zozobra plays a curious role in the Santa Fe Fiesta. For some Santa Feans, the burning is the highlight of the Fiesta, while others do not even consider Zozobra to be a legitimate part of the celebration. Several Santa Feans with whom I spoke, including the Fiesta queen and a member of the De Vargas Cuadrilla, perceived the Zozobra burning as an event that coincided with the Fiesta but was not in actuality a part of the Fiesta. They perceived the change from Friday to Thursday night as further evidence that Zozobra should be viewed as a separate event from the Fiesta. There was a tendency for individuals who saw the Fiesta as a primarily religious or historical celebration to dismiss the Zozobra burning as unrelated to the Fiesta, while those who perceived the Fiesta as more of a civic celebration embraced Zozobra as an important part of the Fiesta. The modern-day Zozobra is sponsored and built by the downtown Santa Fe Kiwanis Club. A five-dollar admission was charged for adults to Fort Marcy Park to observe the burning. The Kiwanis Club donated the proceeds to local charities (Dean, 1999, September 4). Zozobra has provided a way for local non-Hispano, non-Catholic Santa Feans to participate in the Fiesta activities and has historically had a high degree of Anglo involvement.

The Fiesta melodrama has also had a high degree of Anglo participation over the years. The Fiesta melodrama is a theatrical farce that became a part of the Fiesta in 1922 with the production "The Sorcerers of Nambé" by J. D. DeHuff. The melodrama has become an annual Fiesta event that continues to reflect the irreverent attitude of the Anglo art colony of Santa Fe in the 1920s. It leans heavily on social and political satire and contrasts the solemn nature of other Fiesta events with outrageous and often profane humor. Other Fiesta-related events that have attracted strong Anglo participation and support have been the Hysterical/Historical Parade and the Children's Pet Parade.

THE FIESTA AS A RELIGIOUS FESTIVAL

For many Santa Fe Hispanics, the Santa Fe Fiesta is primarily religious in nature. The distinction between the Fiesta as a cultural festival and a religious festival are blurred. As Roger Martinez (1999), a Fiesta Cuadrilla member, expressed, "I can interchange the words culture and religion. They mean the same thing. If you ask me what my culture is, I can say Catholic. If you ask me what is your religion, I can answer, Hispanic."

The 1999 Fiesta queen, Elizabeth Rosa Lovato (1999), stated that "The religious aspect is the most important part of [the] Fiesta. The Fiesta is based on our religion and faith." This focus on the religious aspects of the Fiesta is concentrated on the image of La Conquistadora. She is the central figure in many of the Fiesta activities and she commands the respect of all, including Don Diego de Vargas. Indeed, the patroness and inspiration for De Vargas in the reconquest of Santa Fe was La Conquistadora.

THE FIESTA ENTRADA

The entrada reenactment performed at the Fiesta de Santa Fe probably has stirred more controversy than any other event associated with the Fiesta. The entrada is a reenactment of De Vargas's entry into Santa Fe in 1692, sponsored and staged by the Caballeros de Vargas. The staged event depicted a romanticized version of the scene that occurred when De Vargas and his troops entered Santa Fe in 1692 to reclaim Santa Fe for the Spanish king.

The 1999 entrada was held on Friday of the Fiesta weekend. De Vargas entered the Plaza with his troops and handed a cross to an actor portraying a Pueblo Indian leader, saying, "As a symbol of our peaceful intentions, please accept this." In the reenactment, the statue of La Conquistadora looked on as De Vargas took possession of the city to the sound of trumpets. De Vargas exclaimed, "Pueblo Indians of New Mexico, I have been sent to you by the King with full pardon for all of you. The only condition is that you return to the Catholic religion. The Holy Mother Church will receive you back as a good mother." The Indian representative replied, "Don Diego de Vargas, the return of the Spanish is sure to have happened even though we had hoped you would never come back [laughter], but you have come back and we will try to live in peace with each other. Your religion is our religion. We too love peace. As a sign of our intention, I ask the Padre to bless my children."

This exchange portrayed De Vargas's return as well mannered, and the process as almost a cordial exchange of power. It contained historical inconsistencies and omissions, such as the long verbal tirade hurled at the Spaniards by the Pueblo inhabitants of Santa Fe, or the many hours of negotiation that took place between De Vargas and Pueblo leaders during this visit. More significantly, the second return of De Vargas in 1693 was virtually ignored.

The extent of the historical revisionism is summarized in the narration that preceded the ceremony:

> The Spaniards after the Pueblo Revolt returned in 1692, a humbler people. They no longer considered themselves conquerors and overlords but partners to the Indians in the settlement of this beautiful but harsh land. The Pueblo Indians in turn had come to realize some of the benefits of being exposed to the larger world and welcomed the Spaniards. Both peoples desired peaceful coexistence. God saw this as good and blessed it. Since 1692, neither one people conquered nor was another people subjected, but from the interchange of two cultures was one greater New Mexican culture born, marked by similarities in food, art, architecture and religious belief. We acknowledge the ties that bind us together in an unbreakable bond of solidarity with each other, our God, and the land we love. Through this Fiesta, we expand the circle of friendship to all people who have come to make Santa Fe their home.

The closing narration reinforced the idea of a peaceful reconquest:

> Fellow citizens and visitors to the annual Santa Fe Fiesta, you have just seen reenacted the dramatic Entrada of our hero, the peaceful conquistador, Don Diego de Vargas. This heroic and humane Captain-General and Governor sent to the ancient Kingdom of

New Mexico performed a historic feat right here in this historic city. He could have come up with upraised sword and by force of superior Spanish arms and soldiers could have forced the surrender of this capital city of Santa Fe, but no, he was more than just an ordinary Spanish leader. Captain-General De Vargas was a virile and devout Christian and soldier. He preferred to ask the help of divine providence in the peaceful and challenging resettlement, which he envisioned, knowing full well the future value of such an unprecedented peaceful repossession. But the story of the resettlement of New Mexico does not end suddenly with today's colorful and dramatic pageantry, the history of our ancient city of Holy Faith is being made even now and it will continue as long as there is human life and a Christian spirit of faith.

THE FIESTA MASSES

The three major masses of the 1999 Fiesta were the De Vargas mass that was held at 6:00 A.M. on Friday, September 10, considered by many the opening of the Fiesta; the Pontifical Fiesta mass that followed the solemn procession featuring La Conquistadora on Sunday; and the Thanksgiving mass in St. Francis Cathedral, held on Sunday evening, just prior to the candlelight procession to the Cross of the Martyrs.

The masses were colorful services that included the presence of De Vargas and his Cuadrilla, the Fiesta queen and her court, Fiesta Council members, mariachi musicians, and the Fiesta participants. La Conquistadora occupied a prominent place at the altar during each of the services. Santa Fe Archbishop Michael J. Sheehan presided over the masses.

These masses were almost exclusively attended by Hispanics. Few participants with Anglo or Indian physical characteristics attended the services.

Archbishop Sheehan emphasized during the Pontifical mass that the origin of the Fiesta was religious. The theme of his sermon was centered on forgiveness and reconciliation. He stressed that bigotry in any form was anti-Catholic.

Perhaps the most notable controversy that occurred during the 1999 Fiesta took place at the Thanksgiving mass in St. Francis Cathedral, before the candlelight procession that was the final event of the Fiesta.

The sermon was given by Father Hilaire Valiquette, a Franciscan priest from the mission church in Peña Blanca, New Mexico. The church was full for the mass, marking the end of the Fiesta. People entering the church were given a candle and a clear plastic cup with a hole cut through it to slip over the candle flame so it would not blow out when people marched to the Cross of the Martyrs following the mass. La Conquistadora stood at the front, right-hand side of the altar dressed in an Indian skirt and shawl.

Father Hilaire spoke of the Fiesta as commemorating De Vargas's reclamation and the bringing of the Holy Cross to Santa Fe. However, he said, embedded in the Fiesta are signs of contradiction. He characterized the Fiesta as representing ambiguity. He stated that the Fiesta is an excellent time for reflection about how we are full of contradictions and self-importance. He addressed the Fiesta court, saying, "What we celebrate today contains much injustice and pain. Let us give up our domination. We worship domination. Let go of feeling we are above others and self-righteousness. Our image of the Fiesta is one of military invasion but was it good for the people we invaded? Is it right because we are superior technologically or because we feel morally superior?"

Father Hilaire added that the Spaniards had come to conquer and took the land that was later taken by the United States in an unjust war, and that today the Spanish and Pueblo cultures were endangered by Anglo invaders. He said, "Other cultures do not exist for our entertainment. This is not a Disneyland!" He added, "Victory is false if it is at the expense of other people. The cross is not a sign of victory. We are not above others. Jesus did not come to dominate. All the people we thought we could conquer, we have to learn to live with in peace."

The reaction of some of the central figures in the Fiesta indicated mixed feelings about the sermon. Fiesta Queen Elizabeth Lovato (1999) stated that the sermon was "very inappropriate." She said, "He didn't have the full understanding of our culture. He was stereotyping the Hispanic view of what the Fiesta is." She added, "It was upsetting. Everyone was a little distraught about it. We felt it was too negative. We wanted to focus on harmony."

Tommy Trujillo, the 1999 De Vargas, commented:

He sounded like someone who came from a totally different part of the world. He thought, 'Look at these guys dressed up, bragging that we took the land.' That's not what it's all about. That's not what we're about. I'm sure he didn't see the Entrada and see the way we presented ourselves in the church. He probably didn't even know we went from school to school. It's kind of sad it had to end that way. We put a lot of time into this. We wanted different words in the sermon.

The tension and controversy that surrounded Father Hillaire's sermon cut to the core of the Fiesta's dual nature and a most delicate question: Is the Fiesta a cultural festival that is a source of Hispanic pride, or a reminder of cultural domination?

THE SOCIAL CONSTRUCTIONISM OF THE SANTA FE FIESTA

If social constructionism is transferred through cultural contexts to serve the dominant forces in a given society, then certainly it will have an impact on how historical events are perceived. For example, in the case of the Santa Fe Fiesta, if the current dominant culture in the city were Pueblo Indian, it is doubtful that the arrival of De Vargas would be viewed in the same terms, or if it would be acknowledged at all.

In attempting to answer the question of whether the reconquest of Santa Fe in 1692 and 1693 was "good" or "bad," it is useful to keep in mind the concept that "truth" is a product of competing interpretations and that it is given birth from contextual frameworks (Witkin, 1999).

Opinions concerning the appropriateness of the Fiesta celebration range from Professor Suina's depiction of the Fiesta as a "put-down" celebration, to the 1999 entrada speech that characterized the reconquest as an act of "peaceful coexistence" and the Fiesta celebration as a reminder of "our bond of solidarity with each other, our God, and the land we love." Differing viewpoints concerning the nature of the Fiesta will continue to exist. However, in the sense that the Fiesta remains an important touchstone for Santa Fe Hispanic historical and cultural identity, it will be important for the local Hispanic culture to continue to celebrate it as a source of cultural pride and unity rather than emphasizing any negative connotations.

Table 5. 1999 Santa Fe Fiesta Schedule of Main Events

Date	Event
June 6, 1999	Corpus Christi Procession
August 6, 1999	Royal Ball at La Fonda Hotel
August 14, 1999	Historical lecture at Rosario Chapel
September 4, 1999	Fiesta opening ceremonies
September 5, 1999	Pre-Fiesta show, night parade
September 6, 1999	Old Santa Fe Trail run/walk
September 7, 1999	Special Fiesta City Council meeting
September 8, 1999	*El concierto de mariachi* (mariachi concert)
September 9, 1999	Burning of Zozobra
September 10, 1999	De Vargas mass, entrada reenactment
September 11, 1999	*Desfile de los Niños* (children's pet parade), *La Merienda de la Fiesta* (historical fashion show), *Gran Baile de la Fiesta* (Fiesta Ball).
September 12, 1999	Solemn procession, Pontifical Fiesta mass, *Desfile de la Fiesta* (Historical/Hysterical Parade), closing ceremonies, mass of Thanksgiving and candlelight procession.

CHAPTER FIVE

Santa Fe Hispanic Art and Cultural Identity

The study of Santa Fe Hispanic art and aesthetics provides insight into Santa Fe Hispanic cultural identity and how it is reflected and communicated. The exploration of aesthetic communication is valuable in gaining a more intimate understanding of the attitudes and values that have shaped and continue to influence the Santa Fe Hispanic image and social environment.

Hispanic Art in Santa Fe: A Historical Overview

The first Spanish colonists who accompanied Juan de Oñate to northern New Mexico in 1598 encountered difficult living conditions. Few of the amenities that they were accustomed to having in Mexico and/or Spain were available. Their lot did not improve during much of the seventeenth and eighteenth centuries. They were inhabitants of a remote frontier outpost, far removed from the seat of power in Mexico. Spanish colonists had to depend primarily on their own resources, as imports from Mexico were expensive and infrequent.

The isolation of the Spanish colonists led to the development of a unique folk culture in Santa Fe and northern New Mexico. The artwork produced in this environment has been called "the most important manifestation of folk art in this country, and is in fact the only non-Indian religious art native to it" (Shalkop, 1987, p. 3).

Spanish colonial art was primarily religious in content. The art reflected the importance of the Catholic faith in the identity of the culture. Mather (1983) wrote that these works of art were more than just pleasant luxuries for the Spanish colonists. These objects were "cultural necessities" that carried great symbolic weight. Spanish colonial art maintained the colonists' connection with their roots, their community of origin. The importance of these works of art was magnified, given the remoteness of their environment and the need for the colonists to maintain a link to their faith and to their cultural identity.

Another important function of Spanish colonial art was the use of this art as an instructional tool for the church in the religious conversion of the Indian natives. These visual images were especially important given the language barrier between the Spaniards and the Pueblo people. Art pieces were utilized to convey through symbolism the religious concepts of Catholicism that could not be transmitted verbally (Mather, 1983).

Many of the early Spanish colonial artists who produced religious pieces were missionaries who generated the art themselves to fulfill the spiritual needs of their community. Some of the clerics/artists had been trained in Mexico by monasteries in the techniques of producing decorative and religious arts. However, most of the religious art produced in Spanish colonial New Mexico was by untrained folk artists for community needs (Rosenak and Rosenak, 1998).

Certainly, the Spanish colonial art of New Mexico was strongly influenced by the Spanish and Mexican art traditions. However, these influences were transformed and became unique in the frontier New Mexico environment. Some of the factors that were most responsible for the development of this transformation were the shortage of materials for creating art, such as canvas and paints, as well as the lack of traditionally trained artists in the region. Essentially, Spanish culture was filtered through Mexico and then to New Mexico and pared down to its basic elements by the lack of resources and the struggles of life among the Spanish settlers.

FORMS OF SPANISH COLONIAL ART

Perhaps the earliest forms of Spanish colonial art produced in New Mexico were religious images, which were painted on the walls of newly constructed mission churches. These paintings would have followed the tradition of wall paintings in Mexican churches during the sixteenth and seventeenth centuries.

Paintings done on prepared animal hides began to appear following De Vargas's reconquest in 1692–93. These hide paintings had an advantage over the earlier wall paintings in that they could be transported for worship services or for instructional purposes. The use of hides by the Spanish colonists probably resulted from the influence of their Spanish roots. Spain had long used leather for painting and tooling since it was introduced by the Moslems in the twelfth century (Mather, 1983).

Imported art from Mexico was highly valued in New Mexico and was often seen as possessing higher value and quality. However, the difficulty in obtaining this art and the possibility of its damage during transport made locally produced art a necessity.

Several forms of Spanish colonial art developed in northern New Mexico as time went on. One of the most popular was the "*retablo*." Originally, retablos were painted altar screens that became popular art pieces as more and more permanent churches were built in New Mexico (Mather, 1983).

The term *retablo* also referred to devotional images painted on flat wooden surfaces. These paintings were common in Spanish colonial households and were often a part of home altars (see Figure 11). Their use probably was derived from the larger church-altar screens with which they shared their name (Shalkop, 1967).

"*Bulto*" refers to a three-dimensional carving in the round, which was also popular with the Spanish colonists. These carvings of religious figures and images were usually carved in sections from the soft wood of the cottonwood tree. Some were painted and/or varnished and others were not (see Figure 12). Bultos were common in homes and churches and were also used in Penitente rituals as figures of worship. These wood carvings were highly personalized. They sometimes possessed wigs of human hair and had their own wardrobes (Shalkop, 1967).

Bultos and retablos were referred to as "*santos*" by the Hispanic community. The term *santo* is used to describe a sacred art image. A "*santero*" is the artist who creates the santo. In recent times as more women have become involved in santo making (in the past, women often assisted husbands and fathers, but their work was credited to the male's name), the term "*santera*" has appeared. A "*santeria*" is the workshop in which the santos are made (Shalkop, 1967).

Santos were often not only utilized in worship, but were called upon for intercession. For example, santos portraying Santa Barbara were believed to have power to protect against lightning, San Isidro santos

Figure 11. Traditional New Mexican Retablo. Example of a traditional New Mexican devotional retablo painted on a flat wooden surface. Courtesy the Museum of New Mexico, #147088.

assisted farmers with their crops, and San Ramón Nonato images could assist women in childbirth. Santos were at times rewarded for answering petitioners' prayers with new wardrobes or gifts, or thanksgiving prayers. A santo might also be reprimanded for lack of assistance by being turned to face a wall or being stored until the request was granted. Santos often played an important role in religious celebrations, when they were brought out of the owner's residence to participate in public celebrations (Shalkop, 1967).

The art of Santa Fe and northern New Mexican santeros and other artists gradually developed its own character, shedding Spanish and Mexican influences and gaining a local flavor. The locally influenced folk art was a response to the colonists' needs and sensibilities and it became less and less swayed by external artistic standards (Mather, 1983).

Figure 12. New Mexican Bulto, mid-1800s. Traditional style bulto Nuestra Señora made by Rafael Aragon in the mid-1800s. Photo by Kenneth Chapman. Courtesy the Museum of New Mexico, #57564.

PUEBLO INDIAN INFLUENCE ON SANTA FE HISPANIC ART

The Pueblo Indian people and the Spanish colonists influenced each other's cultures in a variety of ways. In addition to the intermixing of foods, language, and intermarriage, blending also occurred in art.

Ramon A. Gutiérrez (1991) theorized about how the Pueblo Indian culture influenced Spanish colonial art. He stated that Spanish missionaries attempted to make their Catholic God more suitable to the Pueblo people they were trying to convert by depicting God in artistic images as holding Pueblo power symbols such as lightning or arrows that were the Pueblo weapons of war. The Spanish God was also shown on occasion to be holding a heart, which to the Pueblo people symbolized the source of life and breath. Santos produced during this period sometimes contained Pueblo Indian nature symbols such as native animals with Pueblo religious importance.

The attempt that the Spanish missionaries made to integrate the Christian religious images with images of the Pueblo "*Katsina*" (the cloud spirits or ancestral dead) is a particularly dramatic example of the synthesis of Spanish colonial and Pueblo religious images. According to Pueblo religious beliefs, the Katsina spirits were manifested in fog, snow, dew, clouds, and mist. Katsina spirits were also referred to by the Pueblo people as the "rain spirits." The Spanish colonial art and architecture during this period reflected how the Franciscans wanted the Pueblo people to identify the saints and Catholicism with the Katsina spirits. Gutiérrez (1991) cited examples of this borrowing of Katsina symbolism in Spanish colonial aesthetics. The belfry of the Zía church, the church facades at Laguna and Santo Domingo Pueblo, and the churchyard gate at Taos Pueblo utilize the cloud motif that was so important to the Pueblos. Gutiérrez (1991) also referenced the *reredos* (ornamental screens that stood as backdrops for the main altar and to divide space within the church) as invoking the Katsina by depicting the image of God surrounded by clouds. The depiction of spiritual figures and themes surrounded by clouds is certainly not unique to the Pueblos. However, this symbolism utilized by the Spanish may have aided them in presenting their religious messages to the Indian people.

THE SANTA FE ART COLONY

New immigrants dramatically influenced the nature of the art scene in Santa Fe. These were the Anglo artists from primarily the eastern United States. They were among the first Anglo-Americans to settle in the Santa Fe and Taos areas. By the early 1900s, Santa Fe was gaining a reputation among American artists from the East as an interesting place in which to work, and many of the artists who visited the area decided to remain (Robertson, 1974).

The Anglo artists were drawn to Santa Fe and Taos by the natural scenery, the unique quality of the luminous light, and the area's isolation. As Sylvia Rodriguez (1989) stated, "It promised the quintessential frontier experience, vast desert-mountain spaces, wild but noble savages, and unlimited freedom. Fed by a generation of dime store novels, the painters' imaginations in turn produced the visual component for what would become the Taos-Santa Fe mystic" (Rodriguez, pp. 80–81).

A number of the Anglo artists who migrated to Santa Fe came west for health reasons. Some were victims of World War I gas attacks or suffered from tuberculosis and were drawn to the dry, arid climate of New Mexico (Ellis, 1993).

Several of the Anglo artists in northern New Mexico during the early 1900s were trained illustrators who were enamored by the image of the Pueblo Indian as a romantic vision of a time in the past. The painted images they produced also struck a chord with the public throughout the rest of the United States who saw the Pueblo Indian in the romantic role of the "noble savage," free from the pressures and restraints of the industrial revolution taking place in the Anglo world (Udall, 1987). The romanticizing of Indians was not limited to the Pueblo people. The Santa Fe Railroad's image of a Plains Indian chief or the later image of the blue-eyed Navajo boy on the side of Navajo trucks are but a couple of examples of the allure of Indian images in the Anglo-American imagination. Stylized, transcendent images of Santa Fe were an extremely effective form of unintentional tourist promotion and fueled the beginnings of the Santa Fe tourist industry. The Museum of New Mexico, which has promoted Indian and Hispanic artists over the years in Santa Fe, also supported Anglo artists in a variety of ways. The Museum provided studio space and opened a fine arts building in Santa Fe in 1917 to exhibit Santa Fe artists' works. Edgar L. Hewett, the director of the Museum of New Mexico during this period, encouraged Anglo artists from the eastern United States to visit Santa Fe in order to create an art scene (Udall, 1987).

During the 1920s and 1930s, the Santa Fe art colony became established and a number of small galleries were established. Although it was not easy for the Anglo artists to support themselves financially, and many of them had to supplement their incomes by relying on other skills to bring in cash, they established a foothold in the community and helped to shape the character of Santa Fe (Udall, 1987).

Santa Fe captured the imagination of a number of artists and writers during the late 1800s and the 1900s. As English author D. H. Lawrence wrote, "The moment I saw the brilliant, proud morning shine high over Santa Fe, something stood still in my soul, and I started to attend. . . . In the magnificent fierce morning of New Mexico one sprang awake, a new

part of the soul woke up suddenly, and the old world gave way to a new"
(Eldredge, 1986, pp. 152–53).

Santa Fe's praises were sung by a number of well-known writers
including Carl Sandburg, Willa Cather, Mary Austin, and D. H.
Lawrence. The transcendent nature of Santa Fe that they described also
proved irresistible to artists who flocked to Santa Fe and Taos, drawn by
the splendor of the natural light that illuminated northern New Mexico.

The roster of artists who came to paint in the region was impressive.
Among the most famous were Andrew Dansburg, Randall Davey, Gustave
Baumann, Will Shuster, and Mardsen Hartley (Udall, 1987).

The artist who is most closely associated with Santa Fe and northern
New Mexico for the American public is Georgia O'Keeffe. O'Keeffe first
visited Taos in 1929. She soon began to paint in the northern New Mexico
area during the summer months and she finally became a resident of
Abiquiu, New Mexico, in 1949 (Udall and Connors, 1986).

O'Keeffe's paintings of skulls, hills, flowers, and crosses have become
synonymous with New Mexico to many people. One of the most popular
current attractions in Santa Fe is the Georgia O'Keeffe Museum, which
exclusively features her work.

Just as the Spanish colonial aesthetic sensibilities affected the Pueblo
Indian world, the Anglo-American immigration also profoundly impacted
Santa Fe Spanish colonial art. The arrival of traders on the Santa Fe Trail,
who took advantage of the Mexican government's open trading policies,
and particularly the coming of the railroad in the 1880s, had a dramatic
impact on the production of santos in the Santa Fe area. The area was
flooded with mass-produced, plaster-of-Paris religious images. Had it not
been for the Penitentes, santo-making might have become a forgotten
tradition. Many locals became enamored with the new religious images.
However, the Penitentes preferred the traditional santos for their Passion
figures during Holy Week (Rosenak and Rosenak, 1998).

Another important factor in the decline of santo production in Santa
Fe was the arrival of the French Bishop Jean Baptiste Lamy in 1851. He
and his group of foreign clergy saw Spanish colonial art and architecture
as of inferior quality and sought to replace it in the church with more
European-influenced aesthetics (Mather, 1983).

Shimmel (1986) wrote that after the United States occupation, Anglos were elevated to the position of the dominant culture in New Mexico. The Anglo infatuation with Pueblo culture as being in the "noble-savage" category relegated the once culturally dominant Hispanic population to the lowest status among the three groups of Anglo, Indian, and Hispanic.

Rodriguez (1989) suggested that Indian portraits produced by the Anglo art colony were not realistic portraits of everyday life, but instead, the Indians were portrayed as "Ideal types in harmony with Nature, caught at some pristine, eternal moment" (p. 83). Hispanics were not seen in the same light by the Anglo artists or by the Anglo-American public as a whole. Hispanic art was relegated to a position in which it was viewed as not as elevated or "pure" as Indian art or as sophisticated as Anglo-American art. Rodriguez (1989) referred to this situation as the "tri-ethnic trap" in which Hispanics found themselves, "conquered, dispossessed, dependent, ghettoized, and above all, witness to the Indian's spiritual and moral elevation above them" (p. 87). This "tri-ethnic trap" helped to shape "Hispanophobia" or anti-Mexicanism rooted in the beliefs inherent in the Manifest Destiny doctrine and legitimized by the Mexican War (Rodriguez, 1989).

Hispano art was seen by many in the dominant Anglo culture of the early 1900s as "folk art" as opposed to "fine art," and Hispanos creating this art were viewed as artisans as opposed to true artists. Nunn (1998), in her study of Hispano artists involved in the United States' Works Progress Administration programs during the 1930s and 1940s, wrote about Anglo-American attitudes concerning Hispano art in New Mexico. She commented that the Protestant, northern European sensibilities and aesthetics brought by the Anglo population after the 1848 U.S. occupation made it difficult for Hispano art and culture to be understood or appreciated. Nunn (1998) wrote:

> Anglos felt the traditional arts in churches and homes, the result of the Nuevo Mexicano artistic legacy adapting and evolving over centuries, were "crude," "primitive," and "grotesque." The Cristo crucificados were too bloody. The Penitente sect was simultaneously horrifying and fascinating. Once again, Hispano culture was perceived as exotic, pagan, and foreign. (p. 16)

These perceptions of Hispano art persisted throughout the early twentieth century and were evident in the 1930s and 1940s following the Depression, when the United States government's Federal Works Programs were administered in New Mexico.

It is important to note that not all Anglo-Americans shared this attitude toward Hispano art. A number of Anglo-Americans made important contributions toward the preservation and appreciation of Hispano art, as exemplified by artist Frank Applegate and writer Mary Austin who founded the Spanish Colonial Arts Society in 1925. Other organizations that were comprised mainly of Anglo-Americans that contributed to the Hispano arts included the Historical Society of New Mexico, founded in 1859, the Old Santa Fe Association, and the Museum of New Mexico. These organizations are examples of the important role Anglo-Americans have played and continue to play in the Hispano art scene.

THE WPA FEDERAL ART PROJECT

During the Great Depression in the 1930s, U.S. President Franklin Delano Roosevelt instituted a massive national program to put American citizens to work across the country by upgrading the nation's roads, infrastructure, and buildings. Part of this program was targeted at employing artists across the United States. One of the programs that had the most impact on New Mexican artists was the Works Progress Administration's Federal Arts Project, which was initiated in 1935 as a work relief program (Shimmel, 1986).

Many Santa Fe artists participated in this program. Hispano artists worked mainly in traditional formats such as tin, iron, weaving, and wood. Not only did Hispano artists produce art works under the program, they also set up vocational schools to pass along these skills to others. In 1936 there were twenty-eight vocational schools in eight counties in New Mexico. Despite this activity by Hispano artists under the WPA program, they are hardly mentioned in historical or government records (Nunn, 1998).

Nunn (1998) attributed the downplaying of Hispanic artists' contributions to the "prejudicial attitudes" of the period. She elaborated that local Anglo artists belonging to the Santa Fe and Taos art colonies were often cited for their contributions during the program while Spanish-speaking artists were seldom mentioned by name or given specific credit.

Nunn (1998) wrote, "They [Hispano artists] are more often referred to as: naive, native, peasant, quaint, uneducated, untrained people who engage only in 'leisure' activities involved in making handicrafts" (p. 28).

Nunn (1998) stated, "Because most created 'traditional' arts, the Hispana and Hispano artists were considered craftsmen, not artists, and thus not worthy of attention or careful documentation" (p. 3). Only recently, through the research and efforts of academics like Nunn, who organized an art show in Santa Fe in 1999 at the Museum of International Folk Art, showing the work of the "forgotten" Hispano artists during the WPA program, has Hispano art received meaningful attention as art worthy of "serious" consideration. The Palace of the Governors in Santa Fe has also exhibited its collection of Hispano WPA art in recent years, contributing to a resurgence in interest.

THE SANTA FE SPANISH MARKET

The Santa Fe Spanish Market was first organized in 1925 under the auspices of the Spanish Colonial Arts Society, which was developed under the direction of Frank Applegate and Mary Austin. The Society was formed to promote the local Spanish art that had been historically underrepresented. The idea was to display and sell Hispano art during the Santa Fe Fiesta. The Spanish Market became an annual event in Santa Fe until the mid-1930s when it ceased following the deaths of its founders Applegate and Austin in the early 1930s (Shimmel, 1986).

The 1940s were a time of relative inactivity for the Hispanic arts scene in Santa Fe. In addition to the demise of the Spanish Market, the WPA Federal Arts Project ended and Santa Fe, along with the rest of the nation, turned its attention to World War II. Despite the lull in the local Hispanic art scene, basic cultural shifts were taking place in the Hispanic community during this period. The impact of the war and the G.I. Bill benefits following the conflict had a profound effect on Hispano cultural identity. Hispano veterans were returning home with more access to higher education, home-ownership opportunities, and a wider perspective.

In 1952, E. Boyd became the curator for the newly formed Spanish colonial art display at the Museum of New Mexico. Her job as curator inspired her to reestablish the Spanish Colonial Arts Society. In 1965, the

Society reestablished the Spanish Market with only eighteen exhibitors (Shimmel, 1986).

From 1972 to the present, Spanish Market has taken place on the Santa Fe Plaza during the last weekend in July. In 1999, the Spanish Market exhibited the work of 284 artists and drew over forty thousand people (Davila, 1999, July 25).

The Spanish Market expanded to include a Winter Market in 1989 during the first weekend in December. Since 1981, the Spanish Market has included a youth exhibitors' division during the Spanish Market in July, featuring over fifty young Hispano artists (Padilla, 1999).

Since 1985 the annual Spanish Market has also been complemented by a Contemporary Hispanic Market, which allows Hispano artists not working in the traditional forms, required to exhibit in the traditional Spanish Market, to display their work. The Contemporary Spanish Market originally began in the courtyard of the Palace of the Governors and has expanded over the years to occupy an entire street near the Santa Fe Plaza.

The traditional Spanish Market, which referred to itself in its 1999 brochure as "the oldest and largest market in the United States for Hispanic artists working in arts and crafts," has a strict screening and selection process for artists wishing to participate. Artwork must be hand-made by the artist in a limited number of traditional forms and be chosen for inclusion in the market by a panel of judges. Many more applicants apply than are selected each year (Padilla, 1999).

For artists working outside the traditional format, the Contemporary Hispanic Market provides a venue for their work. However, in 1999 a controversy arose between the Spanish Colonial Arts Society (which sponsors the Spanish Market) and the Contemporary Hispanic Market, run by a separate organization. In March 1999 the Spanish Colonial Arts Society board decided that the booth space on Lincoln Avenue near the Santa Fe Plaza that had been occupied in previous years by about eighty artists from the Contemporary Hispanic Market, was needed to make room for expanding the Spanish Market and to provide more booth space for traditional artists. This proposal led to a swell of protest from Contemporary Hispanic Market artists who felt they were being pushed aside because their art did not fit into the traditional stylistic format imposed by the

Spanish Colonial Arts Society (Davila, 1999, July 25). Since then, this proposed change has been tabled and the Contemporary Hispanic Market continues to occupy Lincoln Avenue during Spanish Market.

However, in personal interviews that I conducted with contemporary artists during the Spanish Market on July 25, 1999, two dominant themes emerged that were lying just under the surface of the usually amiable relations between the Spanish Market (primarily Anglo in board-member composition) and the Contemporary Hispanic Market (primarily Hispanic in board-member composition).

First, several artists expressed their concern that Hispanic art was viewed with a narrow frame of reference by many people. They voiced a concern that it was difficult for Santa Fe Hispano artists to work in new media or to create pieces that strayed outside of the traditional styles. If Hispano artists did not use religious images in their work, or used materials traditionally associated with "folk" art, it was hard to be recognized or taken seriously.

Secondly, several artists expressed resentment that few Hispanos were in positions of power within the Spanish Colonial Arts Society and that non-Hispanos often dictated what appropriate Spanish art was. It was evident that they felt restricted by the stereotypical conceptions of the kind of art that Hispanos were expected to create.

These comments by the Contemporary Hispanic Market artists in some ways reflected the comments made by Tom Chávez (2000), former director of the Palace of the Governors in Santa Fe, in an interview previously cited. He stated, "My fear is that we don't try to freeze a culture in a place and time because that will kill it." Rudolfo Anaya, prominent New Mexican Hispano author, also stated a similar sentiment, "Cultures are organic, they're constantly changing" (quoted in Garcia, 1999, p. 11).

ART AND CULTURAL IDENTITY:
AN INSIDER VS. OUTSIDER PERSPECTIVE

Santa Fe is unique in the variety of artistic forms and styles that coexist within a city of its size. Canyon Road is a figurative "street paved with art," with a wide spectrum of galleries featuring diverse art styles. Under the portal of the Palace of the Governors on the Santa Fe Plaza, Indian artisans display their wares. Site Santa Fe is a contemporary arts organization that provides a venue for art exhibitions from around the world. A multitude of shops and tourist-oriented businesses display artwork in a vast array of forms. Within this plethora of creativity, one fact remains: Santa Fe is a tourist town and art commerce is a major contributor to the local economy.

In the following section, a variety of concepts will be explored relating to art and its relationship to indigenous culture and tourism. These theoretical models can be applied not only to Santa Fe, but also to communities nationally and internationally that promote indigenous art as an economic draw for visitors.

Tourist art is a form of art "produced locally for consumption by outsiders" (Jules-Rosette, 1984, p. 9). It can draw upon traditional, indigenous art styles from its culture of origin or it can create new forms unrelated to its past. In the case of Santa Fe, most tourists seek an "authentic" experience, and Santa Fe art that reflects traditional forms has proven to be the most popular.

Bennetta Jules-Rosette (1984), in her book *The Messages of Tourist Art*, wrote about tourist art produced in Africa and the dynamics and communication between artists and tourists. Several of the concepts she explored have direct application in the examination of the Santa Fe art scene. She discussed the value of art objects in the eyes of tourists as opposed to their value for the native culture. Often the art object is viewed by the tourist as valuable because it is a memento of the tourist's journey and is proof that he/she has been to the location of the art piece's origin. This designation of value may be quite different from the artist's original intention. For example, a santo created by a Santa Fe artist may have specific religious meaning for the artist, but may be viewed by the tourist as a quaint conversation piece that would complement the curtains hanging in the living room back home.

At other times, the artist/producer and tourist/consumer may have a similar understanding and appreciation for the art piece. Examples of these scenarios would be a tourist with knowledge and appreciation of Hispanic/Catholic culture buying a santo from a santero artist or, on the other side of the spectrum, a tourist purchasing a commercial tourist item such as a Santa Fe howling coyote wearing a brightly colored scarf from a Santa Fe artist whose intention is to create popular tourist pieces that he/she believes tourists want. In each of these cases, there is a mutual understanding between artist and buyer regarding the intention and symbolic purpose of the art item.

An important aspect of the popularity of Santa Fe as a tourist center is the image of "authenticity" that it has created as a city in which the past is still accessible. That is, Santa Fe is a place "frozen in time." Artwork that captures this illusion is particularly popular with tourists in Santa Fe. Santa Fe artists and craftsmen will often purposely create a "weathered" look to their work in order to capture this feel. Jules-Rosette (1984) wrote that tourists often are on a quest to capture remnants of the past and to discover authenticity, "while accepting the possibility that cultural symbols can be converted into commercial commodities" (p. 4).

The dichotomy faced by Santa Fe Hispanic artists mirror in some ways the split felt by many Santa Feans in general regarding their cultural identity. That is, how does one retain and honor tradition without having it become a straitjacket that does not allow the individual to expand and reach beyond the past? A common attitude prevails that Santa Fe Hispano art is only legitimate as "folk" art and that using contemporary art forms only commercializes and standardizes Hispano art. On the other hand, if Hispano artists continue to work only in traditional formats their work will perpetually be labeled as "folk" and never have the opportunity to be elevated to the "fine" art status enjoyed by other cultural groups.

Antonio López (1999) summed up this dilemma facing Santa Fe Hispano artists when he stated:

> In Northern New Mexico, and in other regions where globalization is encroaching upon traditional, land-based cultures, artists outside the Eurocentric, mainstream art world are being burdened by a subtle oppression of sorts. Their ethnicity overshadows their art. Instead of being judged on aesthetic, philosophical, or even political merit, their works are deigned worthy by virtue of how closely they conform to the institutional perception of a culture's art. (p. 18)

López added:

> Chicanos have a saying, we didn't cross the border, the border crossed us. Similarly, markets defined by ethnicity inevitably frame a culture's expression, establishing boundaries of what is

legitimate expression. If the ethnicity of an artist—in this case a
Hispanic artist—determines the content, the market and the
mode of expression, then how will a culture—let alone the individual— grow and evolve? (p. 18)

Nelson H. H. Graburn (1976) stated, "The labels 'folk' and 'primitive,' have outlived their usefulness and are inadequate or detrimental for
contemporary art analyses" (p. 30).

The Western perspective views folk art as standing still in time and
not moving forward or evolving in complexity. This idea of "eternal repe-
tition" leads to nondevelopment and is not seen as progressive or innova-
tive. This kind of art is basically static, forever in the past (Gablik, 1995).

A number of Santa Fe artists, even those working in traditional formats,
have changed their approach to their art. Rosenak and Rosenak (1998)
pointed out that the convenience, availability, and superiority of modern
materials such as oil-based paints, acrylics, and commercial gesso and varnish
have transformed the methods used by modern-day santeros, but this
contemporary approach does not make their work less authentic than art
using traditional materials. Rosenak and Rosenak (1998) wrote, "Great art
comes from the soul of the artist and reflects his or her idiosyncratic and
personal vision, even though some may say it breaks tradition" (p. 11). As
Griswold del Castillo (1991) wrote, "Attempts to pigeonhole Chicano art
into some ideological or academic agenda has a history of backfiring."

Graburn (1976) contended that culture as well as art inevitably
changes. Innovation is a universal feature in human culture. Although a
culture's art may reflect its past to a greater or lesser degree, it is always
also the product of the present and the outside cultural influences that
create the community in which it is produced. The danger lies, according
to Graburn (1976), in the artist surrendering control of his/her art in order
to please outside buyers and "it is no longer 'his' art, it is 'ours'" (p. 32).

The responsibility for preserving cultural integrity in art lies not only
with the artist but also with the dominant consumer group. Sorrells (1999)
explored the impact of the market on pottery made by Native American
women in New Mexico. She found that the consumer market had affected
the style of the pottery that was produced by Pueblo women and that the

influence of consumers was a powerful factor in changing the traditional Pueblo Indian art form. Bright and Bakewell (1995) contended that art scholars, curators, and critics should challenge the ways that judgments and categories concerning art and cultural boundaries are formed. They gave the example of Chicano culture as being labeled by the dominant American system as either "invisible, criminal or exotic" (pp. 2–3).

Bright and Bakewell (1995) elaborated that the subordination of cultural "others" by the dominant American culture is, in a sense, "a people without a culture, who are nevertheless 'cultured' and exhibit nostalgia for what they themselves have destroyed" (p. 9).

El Museo de Barrio founder Ralph Ortiz stated, "Preserving culture as a vital entity demands that it be liberated from the depersonalizing values of the marketplace, the fashion-mongering of the curatorial process, and the object notion of history" (Bright and Bakewell, 1995, p. 10).

Lucy Lippard added, "Respect for different cultures will bring along with it a greater respect for crafts and commercial and decorative and folk arts and vice versa. But so long as the dignity offered the objects is denied to the people who make or inspire them, cross-cultural consciousness will be an uphill battle for all concerned" (Bright and Bakewell, 1995, p. 11).

The Current Santa Fe Hispano Art Scene

In 1993, the city of Santa Fe conducted a study to assess the impact of the arts on the local population. The report concluded, "The Hispanic community feels disenfranchised from the local arts market" (López, 1998, p. A7). The study also reported respondents stating that there were few opportunities in the city of Santa Fe for Hispanic artists.

In 1990, a group of Hispanic and Indian artists made a presentation to the Board of the Museum of Fine Arts in Santa Fe, stating their concern that the Museum of Fine Arts was not presenting enough work of minority artists. An example of this limited access cited by the protesting artists was the fact that of thirty-four artists represented in alcove shows at the Museum since the shows began in 1986, only one Hispanic and one Indian artist had been exhibited. A Museum board member responded by saying, "The policy needs to change, to be strengthened to specify that these communities not be ignored" (Utgaard, 1990, p. D1).

In a city that has been touted as the third largest art market in the country and in which approximately half of the residents are Hispanic, a feeling persists that Hispano art is not adequately represented.

Of the 185 art galleries listed in *The Santa Fe New Mexican*'s April 7, 2000, Web site's listing of Santa Fe galleries (http://www.sfnewmexican.com /galleries/index/las), only six are listed as representing Hispanic art.

Los Amigos del Museo, a nonprofit foundation that has developed a five-thousand-square-foot warehouse space named "El Museo Cultural de Santa Fe," is attempting to preserve and promote Hispano art in Santa Fe. Miguel Chávez, president of the foundation, said that "for a city that promotes itself as an arts center, Santa Fe has one glaring blind spot: It lacks an exhibition and performance center dedicated solely to Hispanic arts and culture" (Villani, 1996, January 21, p. D1). Through the development of the art center, the organization hopes to provide more exposure for Santa Fe Hispanic artists.

In an effort to examine the status of Hispanic art in Santa Fe, I conducted personal interviews with local Hispanic artists and museum staff to get their impressions about the current state of Hispanic art in the city.

Charlie Carrillo

Charlie Carrillo, one of Santa Fe's most widely known santeros, creates bultos and retablos in the traditional Spanish colonial style, using natural pigments. He is a longtime participant in the Spanish Market and has won many awards for his work. His art has been displayed in museums throughout the Southwest and he is considered one of the masters of the Spanish colonial art style today. In addition to his artwork, Carrillo earned his Ph.D. degree in anthropology at the University of New Mexico in 1996. His dissertation research concerned Hispanic pottery making in New Mexico, a Hispano art form that had been overlooked by prior New Mexico art scholars.

Carrillo (2000) felt that for too long non-Hispanos have defined Hispanic art. The lack of Hispanic input was a prime motivation in Carrillo's dissertation research. Carrillo stated, "It took a dissertation [his own] to prove to Anglo art patrons who thought they knew about our art and culture, that pottery was one of our crafts. I still had a hard time; they just couldn't accept that one of those Hispanics was telling them, who were the experts, what Hispanic people were doing as an art form." Carrillo elaborated, "Now it's an acceptable form at Spanish Market. Pottery was a valuable part of Hispanic life in New Mexico. Saying we didn't make pottery was a way for Anglos to control and tell our people what they think we were."

Carrillo cited the influence on Hispanic art by non-Hispanics with the following example: "If you look at the artists at Spanish Market, instead of painting bright santos, what's happening is when many of them go to Spanish Market, they make them [the santos] look old because that's what's acceptable, that's what a santo is supposed to look like. These aesthetic values are placed on us by non-Hispanics and we've been told year after year, what we have to do to perform to their standards."

Carrillo believed that attitudes had been changing recently. He felt Hispanic artists were beginning to demand more control over their artistic identity. He stated, "I think the tide has finally turned. For the first time in the history of the Spanish Colonial Arts Society, the artists banded together this year. In the last few months we said, 'Wait a second, we have to tell you guys what we are and who we are. We're saying; let us determine what our culture is aesthetically and what are the appropriate ways of making santos.' It's taken all these years and a bunch of artists fighting the system to say, 'Hey, wait a second, this is our culture, this is our art form and we're the ones who should determine the aesthetics of it.'"

Carrillo concluded, "Up until recently, Hispanic art has been determined by a consuming market, by outside influences. It's getting better, but still to some degree the judgments are made by outsiders, they're not made by the people who do the art work, who come from the culture, they come from people outside the culture for the most part."

AnaMaria Samaniego

I also interviewed AnaMaria Samaniego, a Hispana Santa Fe artist, about the current Santa Fe art scene and how it related to Hispanic artists. Samaniego is an active participant in the Santa Fe Contemporary Hispanic Market. She works in monotypes, etchings, collagraphs, pastels, and charcoals.

Samaniego (2000) commented on the challenges facing Hispanic artists who do not work in the traditional, Spanish colonial format. She stated that many of the ideas concerning Santa Fe Hispanic art have come from publicity generated by the Spanish Colonial Arts Society, and these preconceptions have made it hard for Hispanic artists to become more individualistic in their creative process. She also commented that there were not many local outlets for contemporary artists who did not fit into the traditional mold.

Samaniego stated, "The Spanish Colonial Arts Society was a good thing in the past because it brought awareness and support for Hispanic art, but now it can be difficult to break away from the stereotype." She added, "Spanish artists need to grow like in any career and sometimes that may mean breaking away from tradition. We need to keep tradition alive, *retablos* and *bultos*, and that connection with the faith, but also leave room for growth in Hispanic art. We need to be careful not to become a cliché."

Samaniego stated that there was not very much support for contemporary Hispanic art in Santa Fe other than the Contemporary Hispanic Market. She believed there was a real need for more galleries like the former "The Good Hands Gallery" in Santa Fe, which featured both traditional and contemporary Hispanic art, and in Samaniego's words, "shows the wide spectrum of Hispanic art and shows that Hispanic art can come in many, many different forms."

Mural art in Santa Fe has also been a means of communicating Hispanic identity. During the late 1960s and the early 1970s, a group by the name of "Artes Guadalupanos de Aztlán" began painting murals in Santa Fe. The group proclaimed the theme of "Chicano Power" and made a number of political statements. I interviewed two of the original members of this group to obtain their thoughts about art in Santa Fe and Hispanic identity.

Gilberto Guzmán

Gilberto Guzmán came to Santa Fe from California in the late 1960s and began painting murals with Artes Guadalupanos de Aztlán after studying at the San Francisco Academy of Art. Over the years, Guzmán has painted murals throughout Santa Fe and as far away as London. The most recognizable murals that Guzmán has worked on in Santa Fe include the 125-foot mural on the New Mexico State Archives Building on Guadalupe Street, a mural inside the New Mexico State Library on Cerrillos Road, a mural across from the

El Farol Restaurant on Canyon Road, and the mural (now painted over) that stood on a structure on St. Francis Drive in Santa Fe for many years.

In my interview with Guzmán, he discussed the early murals that he worked on during the late 1960s and early 1970s. Guzmán (2000) commented, "It was community art. It wasn't just happening here, but also in San Francisco, LA, Chicago, and New York. Everybody started painting murals. We were all into community trips [and activities]. Whites, Blacks, Chicanos, Asian folks. It was community art."

Guzmán remembered his involvement in the Hispano mural art of the period:

> The first mural we did was on Canyon Road and everybody came down on us; The Historical Society and the police. They didn't want us there. It was Canyon Road and there were all white galleries. We were a threat to their so-called Santa Fe art. Then we did one by St. Francis Drive. That was okay because that was not a white area. As long as we stayed in the barrio, it was okay. Amazingly, those early murals have been published in national magazines and have been used by colleges in their La Raza studies. That's how it started. Art was a power to confront, change and educate. It gave you a positive identity of yourself, that it was not hopeless. Good art lifts your spirits. I'm very happy with who I am because I can speak Spanish, I was able to be a *pachuco*, and I was from the barrios. I think it was very good for me. White folks can't understand it, the closeness of the barrio, you know everybody in the neighborhood. All the stuff I went through, I wouldn't want anybody to go through it but I survived it.

Guzmán believed that the best way to assist young Hispanic artists is to convince them to obtain an advanced education and to enjoy their art rather than just focusing on the business aspect of art. He stated, "We need to teach them [young Hispanic artists] the right perspective. You'll get there, but only if you work at what you're doing. The doors may open for you but you've got to have the product. It's a matter of feeling good, working on yourself, not just painting."

Guzmán had a one-man exhibition of his paintings at El Museo Cultural de Santa Fe in July 2000. The exhibit ran for two months.

Sam Leyba

I also interviewed Sam Leyba, an original member of the Artes Guadalupanos de Aztlán mural group. Leyba is now active in the Santa Fe community as a counselor, working with youth in the arts, and with El Museo Cultural de Santa Fe. Leyba (2000) expressed the need for people in the Santa Fe community to use art as a means of communicating a positive self-identity to Santa Fe Hispanic youth. Leyba commented, "I've taken it upon myself to teach the kids about Chicano culture because there's nobody out there teaching them. For example, Our Lady of Guadalupe is more of a cultural icon these days than a religious one. Kids wear her image on T-shirts but they don't really know much about the religious aspects. They're trying to identify but they don't know the facts."

Leyba felt the Santa Fe art scene was run by economics. He commented, "Today, many artists are looking at making money, which means you'd better paint what the people want to buy. For example, I've never seen a real coyote with a scarf. I've never gotten that close to one, you know, I've seen them but I've never been close enough to see if they're wearing a turquoise scarf or not."

Leyba was working with a group of students at Santa Fe High School on a mural. He believed that the Santa Fe school system was badly lacking in meeting the youth's creative needs. He stated, "The Santa Fe school system was built right after World War I to create workers and it's still stuck there, not to nurture creative minds but to make workers for other people."

Leyba commented on the Santa Fe art scene, "All you have to do is go into the galleries in town. You go into the first one and you say, 'There's some nice stuff in here.' You go into the second one and it's exactly the same. You go into the third one; it's all the same. So actually, good art turns out to be mediocre art because everyone is doing the same thing." Leyba added, "When you ask what's happening in the Santa Fe art scene, it's basically just the same old stuff, the Santa Fe tourists buying the same type of art and more people jumping on the bandwagon. The quality of art is good technically, but it's just not creative. I just haven't seen anything new."

Leyba concluded by reiterating that art can be an effective tool for transmitting Chicano identity but that the attitude should not be "We're proud of being Chicano and everybody else sucks except us." He explained, "It's good to know where you came from, your roots and your culture, but it's also good to know how to learn from others, to share and learn to live together. The last thing I want is for Chicano youth to isolate themselves and be so proud of their culture that they don't want anything to do with Whites or Indians. That's not my intention at all."

Valdez Abeyta y Valdez

Valdez Abeyta y Valdez was director of development and programming at El Museo Cultural de Santa Fe, a Hispanic cultural center and interactive museum. She is also a Hispana contemporary artist and has served on the executive committee of the Contemporary Hispanic Market.

I asked Valdez (2000) to explain the mission of El Museo Cultural de Santa Fe in relation to Hispanic arts. She said, "At El Museo we are not only trying to represent Hispano culture, but also all of its voices, be they contemporary or traditional. At El Museo we are trying to create sensitivity not only for the Hispano but for others as well."

Valdez commented that the amount of Hispano artwork that has been submitted to El Museo is "like an avalanche." She said, "When you think that in the year 2000 there are so few venues for Hispanic artists in Santa Fe and New Mexico, it's sad. If it wasn't so sad, it would be funny. It's hard to even imagine." Valdez attributed the lack of opportunities for Hispanic artists to the economic situation in Santa Fe. "The wealth doesn't lie within the Hispanic community. The Anglos brought their wealth, hence, they have purchased the buildings, and hence, they determined the art venues and the art scene." She stated that often it seems like "Texans come to Santa Fe to buy art produced by Texans, from galleries owned by Texans."

Valdez believed that it is important to expand the notion of Hispanic art beyond the traditional Spanish colonial form in order to attract young Hispanic artists. She elaborated:

Young Hispano artists might say, why should I become an artist? The only thing that sells is the *retablos*. When you look for example at the gang artists, they are artists already; it's just that they have chosen to do a certain kind of art. They already have a sense of balance, aesthetics, dark and light, everything that would qualify them to walk into their first year of college, but they're dropping out of school. Why? Because of the cultural division or lack of identification even in their art. We should be honoring these gang kids who can sit there for 40 or 50 hours working on one piece. We're just not validating who they are and what they're doing.

Valdez concluded by stating, "The difference between El Museo and other places is that you don't have to be dressed a certain way; let's face it, if you walk into other places and you're not a certain kind of person, they're gonna follow you because, 'Oh, they're going to touch,' whereas here at El Museo, everyone is welcome."

Tey Marianna Nunn

Tey Marianna Nunn is the curator of Contemporary Hispano and Latino Collections at the Museum of International Folk Art in Santa Fe. I spoke with Nunn about her thoughts concerning Hispano art in Santa Fe.

Nunn (2000) commented that she had reservations about the term *folk art* as it was used to describe Santa Fe Hispano art:

I tend to be wary of the term folk art especially in relation to Hispano art because it makes it easier to dismiss Hispano art. Folk art is sometimes seen as rustic and quaint but not as art in the European sense. Hispano fine art is often ignored because it is lumped together under the term of folk art.

Nunn gave an example of the difference in perceptions between folk and fine art as it related to the WPA program in the 1930s and 1940s. Hispanos were classified as folk artists and as a result they were paid craftsmen's wages, while Anglo artists were paid higher "artist" wages. She commented:

I would like to see the WPA art exhibited in a fine arts context. It depends on who is interpreting it. If someone else had done the research that I did, the WPA artists might have been portrayed as quaint Hispanic people doing art in poverty in the 1930s and 1940s. It has been a struggle. People have said you can't have paintings in a folk art museum; you can't have furniture and call it fine art. Why not? How about Ames or Shaker chairs, they are considered art, or Queen Ann chairs, those are art. Why would you dismiss Hispano furniture? It's a long and involved battle and it happens every day. These attitudes get swept under the rug and get masked. The battle has not been won; it's not close, unfortunately.

Nunn believed that Hispano art was underrepresented in Santa Fe galleries and museums. She attributed this lack of representation to historical attitudes that labeled Hispanos as "little brown people, who were Spanish-speaking and backward." Whereas the Anglo community elevated Pueblo Indians, the Hispanos of Santa Fe were seen in ambiguous terms. She commented that these stereotypes still persist.

Nunn believed that there are opportunities for the future advancement of Santa Fe Hispano art. She cited the need for more Santa Fe Hispano gallery owners like Ramón José López and Frederico Vigil in order to promote Hispano art. She also stated that the Museum of International Folk Art would be a continuing showcase for Hispano art and there was hope that the Santa Fe Fine Arts Museum would be exhibiting more Hispano art in the future. She also pointed to the openings of the National Hispanic Cultural Center of New Mexico in Albuquerque and the Spanish Colonial Art Society's museum as positive steps. She qualified her optimism with this caveat: "A lot will depend on who is interpreting it [Hispano art]. Will Hispano New Mexicans be in charge? Will Hispano curators be in charge? A lot will depend on the interpretive take."

Frederico Vigil

I had the opportunity to speak with Frederico Vigil (1999) while he was working on a fresco project at the Museum of Fine Arts near the Santa Fe Plaza. Vigil is a renowned fresco artist and Santa Fe gallery owner. His work is prominent locally and admired throughout the world. Although he was on a tight deadline, in which he had to "put the pedal to the metal," he took time to speak to me while he worked.

Vigil said that he wanted to reflect the positive aspects of New Mexico culture in his art, and he could say a lot more in this respect by continuing to support Hispano artists and do his own frescoes rather than by using words. He stated his concern for the "Black Legend," which was perpetuating a negative image of Hispanic culture. Vigil said that Hispanos needed to take back their image and see themselves as sophisticated people and become involved in taking charge of their lives. He felt this was particularly important for the youth of Santa Fe. He noted that kids in local schools are not being taught the positive aspects of their culture and as a result are suffering from an identity crisis.

Vigil stated his belief that Santa Fe Hispanos should become more involved in local cultural events, such as art, music, and literature, and get in touch with their powerful culture that includes a combination of Moorish, Mayan, Indio, and Spanish ancestry.

Vigil expressed his concern that the city was being exploited by outsiders who want to use the Hispanic culture but have no real interest in the people. Vigil commented that some people were afraid of his art because it portrays the power of the Hispano culture. He stated that he noticed the fear some people have of the traditional Hispano culture of Santa Fe. They want the "safe" art and symbols that have been constructed for tourists, but shy away from really getting to know the culture. They prefer Hispanos to remain "invisible."

Ramón José López

Ramón José López is a native Santa Fe artist and the former owner of The Good Hands Gallery in downtown Santa Fe, which featured a wide range of Hispanic artists. López is an artist who works in various formats including santo making, jewelry, and painting. He is a prominent artist who has received the National Heritage Fellowship from the National Endowment for the Arts and is displayed at the Smithsonian Institute.

López (2002) stated that he saw himself as an "ambassador" for the artists he represented and for the city of Santa Fe as a whole. He felt that tourists who buy local art wanted to feel welcomed. Lopez believed that there is a high demand for Hispano art. However, he stated that artists needed to price their work at a price that buyers with limited budgets could afford. He also felt that it was also important for artists to be good in business to succeed.

López commented that all Hispano artists in Santa Fe were in a sense "contemporary artists," despite the fact that they may be working in traditional forms. He stated that the original bultos and santos produced during the Spanish Colonial period were unique and distinctive because of their importance to the people on a personal level. López explained, "The religion was strong and they really believed in San Isidro. You prayed to him, your whole family was involved. The art wasn't produced to make money and this made a difference."

López believed that contemporary Hispano artists needed to continue to explore new directions and not only follow traditional designs. He stated that it is important to have innovation. "How many retablos in the same format can you see? I see myself as a changing artist. You get bored and you need to try something else."

Although López agreed that the number of venues featuring Hispano art in Santa Fe was relatively small, he believed that there was more awareness in recent years by museums and galleries that Hispano art was important.

Conclusions

The role of art in Santa Fe Hispanic culture has been important in defining Hispanic identity from Spanish Colonial times. Art has reflected religious devotion, cultural heritage, and societal attitudes for Santa Fe Hispanics for many centuries.

Santa Fe Hispanic art has been a mirror reflecting changes in culture and identity. The influences of Indian and Anglo culture have been evident in the Hispanic art of Santa Fe.

Self-defined versus other-defined cultural identity is a major issue confronting contemporary Santa Fe Hispanic artists. They voiced a consistent concern that they wished to acknowledge and honor their Spanish Colonial art tradition but, at the same time, they did not wish to be confined or labeled only as "folk" artists bound exclusively by the art forms and expressions of the past.

CHAPTER SIX

Tourism's Impact on Santa Fe Hispanic Identity

Santa Fe had an estimated population of 63,500 residents in 2002. The population of the city is dwarfed by the influx of visitors that make Santa Fe their vacation or convention destination. In addition to economic impacts, this tourism has had a profound influence on the social and cultural dynamics of the city. In this chapter, I examine this influence, particularly as it pertains to Santa Fe's Hispanic cultural identity.

DEFINING AUTHENTICITY IN TOURIST COMMUNITIES

Both tourists and residents in communities that host large numbers of tourists claim a strong preference for authenticity in their interactions. However, according to Kirk (1994), these two groups often have differing views on what is authentic.[1] The core of this difference lies in the perception that tourism itself is often seen as making a place inauthentic since the tourist industry is directed toward outsiders. To be accessed by tourists, indigenous life and customs must often be simplified from their usually complex symbols and practices into a form that is more easily accessible to the outsider.

Santa Fe's Hispanic residents are particularly sensitive to cultural changes that they feel are not in their local control. To interpret these feelings in the framework of authenticity, many Hispanic Santa Feans see their city as becoming inauthentic. Mathieson and Wall (1982) stated that resentment toward tourism tends to be highest in "tourist magnet" areas, where tourism is the principal source of income and where most activities are directed toward supporting the tourist's demands. The indigenous population must feel that it can physically and psychologically absorb the tourist influx without undermining or displacing its own cultural integrity.

Cohen (1988) warned that too much commoditization could change the meanings of cultural products and interactions between tourists and natives and render them meaningless to both visitors and the indigenous population. However, such a gloomy scenario does not necessarily have to become the case. In some instances, a cultural product that has at one time been judged as inauthentic may, at a later time, become recognized as authentic, even by the native population. An example of this transformation can be found in the figure of Zozobra in the Santa Fe Fiesta. Many Hispanic Santa Feans view Zozobra as an authentic, legitimate part of the Fiesta celebrations, although the origin of Zozobra was in no way tied to the original meaning or traditions of the Fiesta celebration.

Not all tourists share the same degree of concern for authenticity in their experience. Cohen (1988) placed tourists into several categories according to their desire for authenticity. He called the first group "political pilgrims," who tend to idealize their destinations and seriously pursue authentic experiences. He labeled the second group "experimental" tourists, who also have strict criteria for authenticity but are not as invested in absolute authenticity as the former group in order to have a satisfying experience. He labeled the third group "recreational" tourists, who possess a more playful attitude of "make-believe" and will tolerate a broader range of authenticity/inauthenticity. Lastly, Cohen (1988) described "diversionary" tourists, who were mostly unconcerned with the issue of authenticity. He stated, "The question here is not whether the individual does or does not 'really' have an authentic experience, but rather what endows his experience with authenticity is his own view" (pp. 377–78).

The quest for authenticity seems to spring from a need in modern society to discover a refuge from the alienation of contemporary life and to find a pristine environment in a somewhat natural form, which is still untouched by industrialization and commercialism. Thus, the fascination of visitors for Santa Fe's adobe buildings and handmade art pieces is understandable.

THE IMPACT OF TOURISM ON NATIVE CULTURES

While tourism can provide a number of economic benefits to locations like Santa Fe, much scholarly literature suggests that wholesale commodification of a region or a culture can have negative repercussions.

Messerli (1995) suggested that research over the past three decades indicated that areas that develop tourism too successfully are often fated to an eventual demise. She explained that when a tourist region draws increasing numbers of visitors and related development, the original charm of the area begins to diminish and it becomes overcrowded, exploited, and loses its appeal for both visitors and residents. As Yogi Berra once commented when referring to a popular New York restaurant, "Oh that place, it's not that popular anymore; too many people go there." This phenomenon is often commented on by locals who fear that their city will be exploited and then thrown on the trash heap of "yesterday's in-spot." A recent example is the city of Aspen, Colorado, which is referred to by many Santa Feans as a precursor of problems to come if the current trend is not abated in Santa Fe. Aspen, now a chic Colorado ski town, became a magnet for the rich during 1970s and 1980s. The popularity of the city drove housing costs up so high that few middle-class people could afford to live there. The town lost much of its original charm as local businesses gave way to high-end shops and restaurants. Aspen is often now cited as an example of what can go wrong when a small city becomes too trendy and overly commercialized. It is not uncommon to see the bumper sticker in Santa Fe, "Don't Aspenize Santa Fe."

In the case of Santa Fe culture, the pressures of tourism are compounded by the presence of state and federal government and two liberal arts colleges in the city. All of these outside influences, while in many ways beneficial, nevertheless effect and exert change on the traditional local culture.

In a scenario that in several ways mirrors some of the recent changes in Santa Fe, Lippard (1999) described certain tourist towns across the United States:

> They are desperately framing and reinventing their histories to make the picture more appealing to those who might buy a hamburger, T-shirt, suntan lotion, Indian jewelry, a plastic seagull, a shell ashtray, or a boat ride. Corporate developers are invading the unspoiled with condos, Burger Kings, and golf courses . . . (p. 60)

This type of tourist development leads to a local labor force that is employed in mainly low-paying, service jobs that support the pricey restaurants, hotels, and assorted amusements designed to lure tourist dollars.

The historical norm has been for the gains from tourism development to be largely enjoyed by outsiders and by a handful of entrepreneurs, rather than benefiting the indigenous populations of tourist destinations.

In response to this dilemma, a Santa Fe City Council ordinance was adopted in September of 2003 to raise the minimum wage in Santa Fe in graduated steps. Beginning in January of 2004 the ordinance would require businesses with over twenty-five employees to pay a minimum wage of $8.50. In 2006 the minimum wage would rise to $9.50 and in 2008 it would be $10.50. Although this ordinance became law on June 24, 2004, it is being challenged in the courts, and its future remains unclear.

De Kadt (1979) observed that local capacity to control tourism development to serve the bigger community generally has been weak, especially when this development is large scale, such as in the case of Santa Fe. He stated, "Outside interests that move in can easily ride roughshod over such limited and often ill-conceived by-laws and regulations as exist; alternately, laws are often enacted after the damage has already been done" (pp. 8–9). The result of the overpowering force of tourism is that often people in the local community whose lives are profoundly affected by the development have little voice in the changes that sweep their environment.

The debate over the benefits and costs that tourism incurs in communities is an international concern. Santa Fe is but one of a multitude of regions that engage in ongoing dialogue and soul-searching regarding this question. A pro-tourist position is held by some who see tourism as a way to bolster marginal economies. The anti-tourist position is held by those who claim that tourism irreversibly changes local culture, and often the revenue that it generates is monopolized by large concerns like hotel chains and airlines (MacCannell, 1976).

Messerli (1995) suggested that the impact of tourism on a community couldn't be neatly categorized into separate categories. She wrote, "Economic impacts spill over into socio-cultural impacts which spill over into political impacts" (p. 3).

In the following section, the impact of tourism on Santa Fe is explored and analyzed as to how these forces have had an effect on indigenous Hispanic Santa Feans.

THE IMPACT OF TOURISM AND DEVELOPMENT ON SANTA FE

Santa Fe is struggling to cope with growing pains. With an expanding tourist population and a resident population projected to reach seventy thousand in the near future, many native Hispanic Santa Feans feel a loss of control over the direction in which their city is headed. They are concerned with the effects of uncontrolled growth and rampant tourism that are changing the nature of their city.

A major concern is maintaining an adequate supply of water for the city's residents. Mayor Larry Delgado cites this issue as one of his top priorities. In a poll conducted by the Santa Fe Quality of Life Committee in January of 2004, 71 percent of Santa Fe residents ranked water shortages, drought, or water quality as the most important problem facing Santa Fe. The Santa Fe area has experienced a number of dry years since 1996, and even though strict water conservation measures have been enacted the situation remains precarious as the drought continues. Among the casualties of the extended drought are Santa Fe's beloved piñon trees and their nuts that have been a delicacy for Santa Feans for generations.

Hanna Rietz Messerli (1995) studied Santa Fe tourism life-cycle models and residents' perceptions. She wrote that there was a general concern among the residents she interviewed regarding a need to control growth and tourism, but there was no consensus as to how and if they could be controlled, and there was not even a commonly articulated definition or explanation of "control." Some of the common questions that Santa Feans grapple with are defining what is changing in their community and what the specific causes are. Santa Fe residents also are concerned with the long-term ramifications of the perceived changes and remedies for curbing these changes.

Messerli (1995) noted that many locals bemoaned the changes that had occurred around the Santa Fe Plaza, which appeared to cater only to the needs of tourists and art collectors. She cited a general longing for "better times gone by," with comments like "Santa Fe used to be a community . . . but now you can't go walking downtown and see someone

Figure 13. Santa Fe Plaza, 1965. Locally owned stores such as Moore's and Anthony's, which catered to local shoppers, have gradually been replaced by tourist-oriented businesses. Photo by Karl Kernberger. Courtesy the Museum of New Mexico, #29026.

you know any more like you used to" (חיי מיה וגו) (see Figure 13).

Linnard (1999) commented:

By 1998, everybody—natives, old timers and newcomers, outsiders and insiders—seems to agree that Santa Fe has changed for the worse in the last 25 years. The city different is now too crowded, too expensive, and either vulgarly cliché-ridden or so tasteful as to be tasteless. (p. 60)

In the film *The Milagro Beanfield War*, directed by Robert Redford and set in a small New Mexican town, the line spoken by actress Sonia Braga sums up the feelings of many Santa Fe natives: "What good is it to have a home town when everyone you know is gone?"

As early as 1983, John Pen LaFarge, a columnist for *The Santa Fe New*

Mexican newspaper, wrote that the downtown area and the Santa Fe Plaza were intended for the use of one and all. He wrote that by 1990, "The Plaza will be of no use except to the tourists and the wealthy who love high-priced shopping." He stated that Santa Fe would become "one of the most exclusively wonderful cities in the United States but for others, not for residents of the city" (Ozen, 1994, p. 71).

According to the Santa Fe Association of Realtors, during the fourth quarter of 2002, the median cost of buying a house in Santa Fe hit an all-time high of $272,000. This figure compares with a national median price of $158,000. In an interview, with *The New Mexican* on October 8, 1999, Mike Loftin, director of Neighborhood Housing Services, a nonprofit group that helps low-income and middle-class people buy homes, said, "It's just amazing that prices have gone up that much. It's scary" (Quick, 1999, p. A-1).

Many Hispanic Santa Feans have equated the rise in tourism with the increasing number of Anglo residents from outside of the region. De Kadt (1979) referred to these people as "settler" tourists who in many regions are still considered tourists because many do not earn their living in the region and they do not share the cultural background of the native population. Lippard (1999) called these newcomers "amenity migrants." She noted that they often display the "drawbridge syndrome," in which they quickly complain about the tourists and other newcomers. Messerli (1995) quoted a Santa Fe County Chamber of Commerce official who explained, "What is it about people in Santa Fe that they always introduce themselves by saying how long they have been in Santa Fe. . . . It's really nutty. . . . The difference between resident and tourist is constantly trying to be established" (p. 147). Messerli (1995) analyzed this phenomenon by stating, "What is particularly difficult to pinpoint is at what point newcomers or transplants perceive themselves as old timers. One could argue that this occurs as soon as individuals have been in the area for an even shorter time than they have. They then try to limit 'newcomers' and those who don't respect Santa Fe's past, particularly Texans and Californians" (p. 147).

The strong demand for housing and the subsequent rising prices and property taxes have made it difficult for many Santa Fe Hispanics to afford to live in Santa Fe or for their children to have a future in the city. More and more Hispanics who choose to remain in the city are being forced to

Figure 14. Trailer Park on Airport Road, south Santa Fe. As housing costs and property taxes have escalated in recent years, more Hispanic Santa Feans have migrated to more affordable mobile home parks in south Santa Fe. Photo by Andrew Lovato, 1999.

the south side of town, outside the city limits into trailer parks or subdivisions. You will not find much of the "Santa Fe mystique" in these areas around Airport Road and Lone Butte (Figure 14).

At the same time, many Anglo newcomers to Santa Fe move into gated communities behind high adobe walls (Figure 15) and live in multistory adobe fortresses or build mansions on Santa Fe's ridgetops, marring the landscape in order to have an inspiring view of the Sangre de Cristo Mountains (Figure 16). The segregation of newcomers and natives is part of the reality of the tricultural harmony of Santa Fe that is flaunted in the local tourist literature.

Local families who have managed to hold on to their homes find themselves land-rich but cash-poor. The development, escalating costs, and high property taxes continue today with no immediate end in sight.

Ray Amenta, a twelfth-generation Santa Fe Hispanic landowner, commented in the film documentary, *La Villa De Santa Fe*, produced by Miguel Grunstein (1995):

I don't see any of my friends in the eastern side of the foothills of Santa Fe, they're gone, they're being flushed out. It saddens me to ask old friends that I grew up with: Where do you live? They honestly and truthfully just tell me, Ray, I live in a trailer down

Figure 15. Quail Run, a gated Santa Fe community, front entrance. This Santa Fe housing complex is fortressed by thick adobe walls and a guardhouse. The residents also have a private golf course on the grounds. Photo by Andrew Lovato, 1999.

there in the south part of Santa Fe by the Penitentiary, Lone Butte, these areas, and I ask them: How did this come to be? And they say, well, they offered us a lump sum of cash for our house and we let it go. People have sold to the outsider, the outsider built these beautiful homes so the cost of real estate goes up. What happens to the taxes? It's exorbitant; it's getting astronomical. So basically you're between a rock and a hard place and you're gonna have to sell cause there's nothing else to do.

SANTA FE TOURISM AND DEVELOPMENT STATISTICAL DATA

The rate of increase in visitors to Santa Fe was reflected in the number of hotel room occupancies since the early 1980s. The number of available hotel rooms in the city climbed from approximately 2,260 to 3,800 between 1980 and 1990. At the same time, the occupancy rates also grew from about 60 percent to 70 percent. Hotel receipts multiplied from 25 million dollars in 1985 to 86 million dollars in 1992 (Wilson, 1997).

Figures in 2002 reported by the Rocky Mountain Lodging Report showed that this upward trend in tourism is continuing. It is estimated that area hotels generate approximately 750,000 nightly room reservations

Figure 16. Ridge-Top Homes, Northern Santa Fe. These ridge-top homes dominate the north side of Santa Fe, much to the chagrin of many locals who believe these structures mar the Santa Fe landscape. Photo by Andrew Lovato, 1999.

annually. This represents a sizable source of income and tax revenue.

The revenue generated from the tourism industry is impressive. Total annual gross receipts consistently top over 100 million dollars for hotels and lodging and over 5 million dollars in lodger's taxes. An even more important contribution to the local economy is the impact that tourism has on the retail trade, which now exceeds 1.6 billion dollars annually (Santa Fe Chamber of Commerce, 2003).

The trend of increasing tourism revenue is expected to continue, with the city estimating 5.5 million dollars in lodger's tax revenue for the 2002–2003 fiscal year. Gross receipts taxes alone are anticipated to generate almost 69 million dollars in 2002–2003 (City of Santa Fe Planning and Land Use Department, 2003).

Art galleries and jewelry shops continue to multiply in the city. Wilson (1997) reported an increase in these businesses from 107 in 1985 to 295 in 1992. It is estimated that by the year 2000 over 320 such businesses will be operating in the city (Santa Fe County Chamber of Commerce, 1999). The rise in tourist-oriented businesses is evident on the Santa Fe Plaza, where businesses oriented toward local consumers have completely vanished.

The plan initiated in the 1920s by the Museum of New Mexico to "touristize" Santa Fe appears to have been a complete success. Particularly since the boom of the 1980s, the tourism industry has come to dominate the Santa Fe economy. City planners and business entrepreneurs encouraged Santa Fe's "City Different" persona during the twentieth century in anticipation of the tourism industry. Certainly, the city's decision in 1957 to enforce adobe-style architecture ordinances in the downtown area was at least in part motivated by the appeal it would have for tourists. A sense of urgency set in during the mid-1950s to preserve Santa Fe's distinctive architectural image. The *New Mexican* newspaper voiced the concern of many local residents when it stated, "Our chief danger lies in the fact that we are fast becoming less and less unique, and more and more like any southwestern community of comparable size" (Wilson, 1997, p. 254).

A political movement spearheaded by novelist Oliver LaFarge galvanized support for a design control ordinance requiring "Santa Fe style" architecture in the downtown area. After much debate and hand-wringing, the Santa Fe City Council passed a building ordinance in the fall of 1957 that endorsed architectural uniformity and planning requirements for construction in areas deemed historic zones in the city (Wilson, 1997).

The rise in tourism transformed the city in many ways. The popularity of Santa Fe swelled not only for visitors but also for people wishing to become permanent residents. Table 6 shows the rise in population during the 1900s.

Table 7 shows the shift in ethnic composition that occurred in Santa Fe between 1970 and 2000. The Census 2000 numbers are interesting in that they show a slight shift in the demographics. Anglo population numbers are slightly down while Hispanic and Indian number rose slightly. The increase in the "other" category is attributable to the change in the U.S. Census reporting form. It allowed people for the first time to mark "two or more races" as an option. Although it is still too early to make any clear assumptions, Census 2000 may foretell a new trend toward a Hispanic majority in the demographics of Santa Fe.

The current economic pressures on Santa Fe Hispanics make living in Santa Fe more difficult as median housing costs soar beyond $270,000. Santa Fe Hispanics find they live in a city that is in danger of becoming completely gentrified except for a few pockets on the outskirts of town (Figure 17).

Table 6: Santa Fe's Population from 1900 to 2000, by Decade

Date	Population	Percent increase
1900	5,603	—
1910	5,073	- 9%
1920	7,236	+ 42%
1930	11,176	+ 54%
1940	20,325	+ 82%
1950	27,998	+ 38%
1960	34,394	+23%
1970	41,167	+ 19%
1980	48,953	+ 20%
1990	55,541	+ 13%
2000	62,203	+ 12%

Table 7:
Ethnic Composition of Santa Fe from 1970 to 2000, by Decade

Year	Hispanic	Anglo	Indian	Other	Totals
1970	26,642 (64%)	13,792 (34%)	1%	1%	100%
1980	26,899 (55%)	20,054 (41%)	838 (2%)	2%	100%
1990	26,302 (47%)	27,492 (49%)	1,000 (2%)	2%	100%
2000	29,744 (48%)	27,300 (44%)	1,373 (2%)	6%	100%

DEBBIE JARAMILLO AND THE 1994 SANTA FE MAYORAL ELECTION

The expansion of tourism and the gentrification of Santa Fe that took place during the 1980s and early 1990s under Mayor Sam Pick's administration were dramatic. Pick's pro-business, pro-development policies gained the support of business interests in the city. However, a growing wave of resentment was also building during this period. Native Hispanics and many long-term Anglo residents began to grow alarmed at the rapid changes engulfing the community. The dismay grew with every new overpriced restaurant or souvenir shop, or property tax increase.

Debbie Jaramillo was elected to Santa Fe's city council in 1988 on a platform opposing resort development and gentrification. She had begun her involvement in politics in the early 1980s when she began fighting a proposed road widening through her West Side neighborhood to be used by vehicles carrying nuclear waste from Los Alamos.

As a city councilor, Jaramillo often was a solitary voice opposing

Mayor Sam Pick's and the city council's pro-development policies. The drive toward more development could not be characterized as simply a racial issue as past Hispanic Santa Fe mayors and city councilors had also participated enthusiastically in the commodification of Santa Fe. Jaramillo was an outspoken critic of uncontrolled development and tourism. She was not seen in a favorable light by many in the local business community. However, her grassroots support among many local citizens grew during her stormy years on the Santa Fe city council. In 1991, Jaramillo ran for mayor of Santa Fe, finishing second to Sam Pick.

As the 1994 mayoral election approached, the development of Santa Fe seemed to be escalating with new venture developments, hotels, and a proposed ski resort expansion. A swell of negative publicity also emerged surrounding Hollywood actress Shirley MacLaine's plan to build a ridgetop mansion on a scenic Santa Fe mountain. The actress purchased thirty-six acres of property on Atalaya Mountain with the intention of having a home in which she could look down at night on the lights of Santa Fe. Many locals complained that this also meant that they would have to look up at the lights of MacLaine's home when they viewed the mountains east of Santa Fe. Public outcry finally led MacLaine to give up her plans to build her Santa Fe home on Atalaya Mountain.

The media during this time period suggested that ethnic and class tensions were rising as perceptions grew that wealthy immigrants were taking over the city.

Jaramillo ran once again for mayor in 1994 opposing front-runner Peso Chávez, a two-term city councilor, who favored pro-business and pro-development policies, and was supported by the former backers of Mayor Sam Pick.

Jaramillo emphasized that the Hispanic population was being displaced, as Santa Fe became a "playground for the rich." She stated in an interview that local Santa Feans were becoming "people living on the outskirts, bussed in to make the beds and shine the shoes and clean the toilets of the rich. We sure can't enjoy that part of Santa Fe because a lot of the economic changes cater to the big buck, while we've got our shopping centers for the locals, that whole downtown has grown with high-end restaurants, shops, boutiques, and galleries" (Grunstein, 1995).

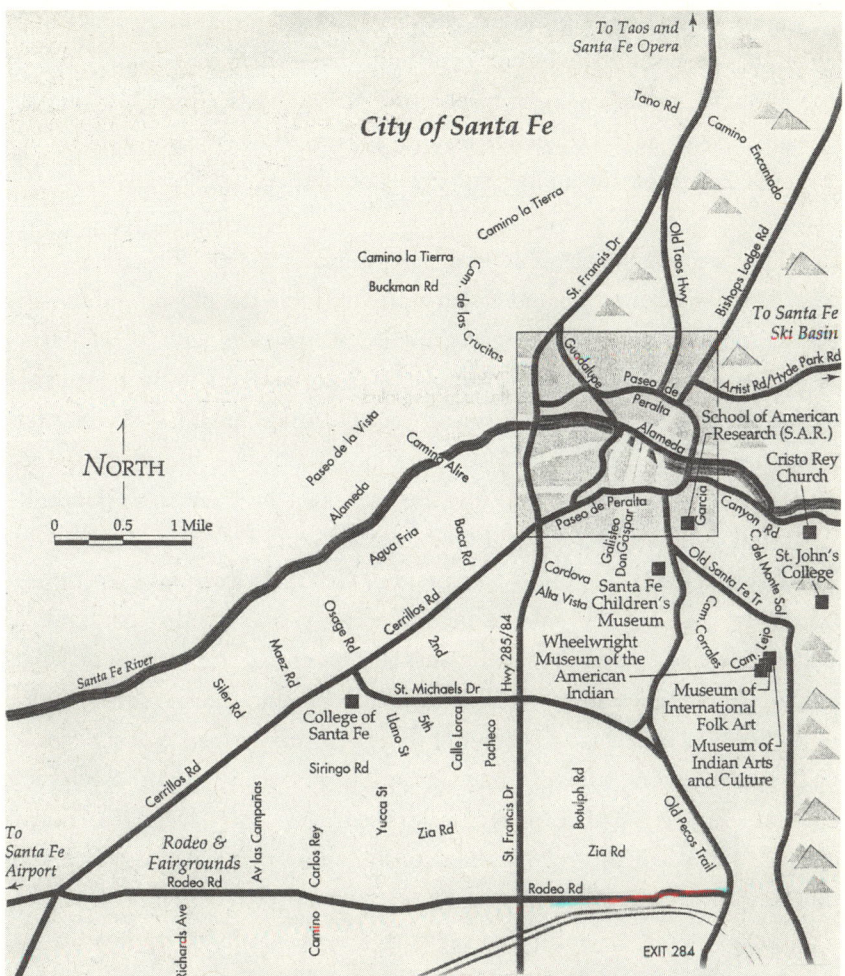

Figure 17. 1996 Map of Santa Fe. As Santa Fe's downtown area has become gentrified in recent years, more Santa Fe Hispanic residents have moved to the southern outskirts of the city and away from the once predominantly Hispanic Plaza area. Used by permission of the City of Santa Fe Convention and Visitors Bureau, 1996.

In March 1994, Jaramillo was elected mayor of Santa Fe in an upset victory despite being outspent by Peso Chávez. The voter turnout was a record-high 59 percent of Santa Fe's eligible voters. A coalition of grassroots Hispanics, liberal Anglos, and older families elected Jaramillo, united in a desire to preserve Santa Fe's character. Bruce Selcraig (1994) wrote for *The High Country News*:

Elderly Hispanic supporters who had almost quit coming downtown because of the tourist onslaught made their way proudly to
Jaramillo's election-night celebration at La Fonda Hotel. Jubilant
and awed at their newly found power, they would politely
approach their champion, embrace her, and cry. (p. 10)

The four years of Debbie Jaramillo's term as mayor of Santa Fe were
marked by confrontation and disharmony between the mayor and the city
council concerning the issues of growth and development, as well as an
assortment of other issues. At times the disagreements grew personal in
nature and the Santa Fe public grew weary of the squabbling. In an interview with *The Santa Fe New Mexican*, almost four years into her administration and a couple of months before the 1998 election, Jaramillo
conceded that curing the social inequities in Santa Fe was a goal that was
still a long way off. Jaramillo commented, "It's real clear that I've concentrated on the low and middle-income class people in this community.
Whether we're talking about housing or jobs or daycare centers or whatever fits in. I think that I've done a lot, but four years doesn't touch the tip
of the iceberg in terms of balancing things" (Neary, 1997, p. A-1).

In the mayoral race of 1998, Jaramillo was pitted against Sam Pick,
who was seen as a promoter of development, and Larry Delgado, considered a middle-of-the-road candidate between the polar opposites of
Jaramillo and Pick. Delgado won the race by a decisive margin.

In retrospect, Jaramillo was portrayed by her political opponents and
pro-business interests as mean-spirited and radical. This stereotype led to
her political decline. However, Jaramillo was seen by many as a voice for
many low-income and middle-class Santa Feans. In the end, Santa Feans
opted for a compromise and a mayor who could perhaps bridge the polar-
ized factions and bring harmony back to City Hall.

The Impact of Development and Tourism on Santa Fe Hispanic Cultural Identity

Ray Armenta, a twelfth-generation Santa Fean, spoke for many longtime
Santa Fe Hispanics when he stated, "All of a sudden, I feel anymore, when
I come to Santa Fe that I'm not really treated anymore like a local, like a

native. I feel like the outsider coming in" (Grunstein, 1995).

Celina Rael de Garcia, former director of the Office of Cultural Affairs for Santa Fe, stated, "I see it as a positive thing that the community is saying, 'I'm angry' because that takes away from the dysfunction that's been going on in Santa Fe where people are saying 'everything's fine.' You know, 'everything's wonderful, *mi casa es su casa*,' and that wasn't true. More traditional people are coming out and saying, it's not okay. I am not less than, I am part of this community and it belongs to me" (Grunstein, 1995).

Father Jerome Martinez y Alire, rector at St. Francis Cathedral, commented in Grunstein's 1995 video documentary *La Villa De Santa Fe*:

> It's overall been that same attitude on the part of some of these newcomers, that we're here to fix, we're here to make better according to our own image and likeness, and that's causing resentment on the part of some natives who say, we don't need to be fixed, we're not a problem to be solved. If you want to dialogue with us, we're willing to dialogue, but we're not willing to be dictated to because of money or because of influence or because of power.

These comments, taken from Grunstein's documentary, reflect the ambivalence that many Hispanic Santa Feans feel today about their cultural identity. Many local Hispanics feel underappreciated, underemployed, and underrepresented. After hundreds of years of being the dominant culture in Santa Fe, a city they founded, the perceived decline of their culture is a bitter pill to swallow. Hispanic culture in Santa Fe, according to Lippard (1999), is "curiously both dominant and subordinate, despite the fact the 'real Santa Fe' is better reflected by Latino than Anglo or Indian culture" (p. 63).

Another issue that must be raised is the question of empowerment within the Hispanic community. That is, are there some members within the Hispanic community who are also responsible for the commodification and the push to "improve" Santa Fe by "fixing" traditional Hispanic culture and values?

Although Pueblo Indian culture is a draw for many tourists, aside from the Indian artisans on the portal of the Palace of the Governors, and the presence of Indian art in Santa Fe museums and galleries, Indian people make up a very small percentage (about 2 percent) of Santa Fe's population. Most Indians live in the outlying pueblos and coexist independently of Santa Fe.

The balance of Santa Fe's population has shifted. The traditional Hispanic majority is not as dominant as in the past.

The public relations notion of Santa Fe as a "melting pot" and a city of "tri-cultural harmony" is not the reality for many local Hispanos who resent the simplification of their culture to "coyote figurines, bright pastel T-shirts, and stylized home decorations" (Kirk, 1994).

Many locals fear losing the aspects of place that make up an important part of the Santa Fe Hispanic identity.

If authenticity is an important consideration for tourists, it is vital to the well-being of the native Hispanic population. As Kirk (1994) wrote, "Identity is linked to authenticity through meaning. If there is stability of meaning, then a group can rely on that meaning as a source of identity" (p. 82). She continued, "An authentic place can be used as a source of identity. If a place becomes placeless through reduction or erosion of its symbols by mass culture, the people who used this place for a source of identity could lose that source" (p. 82).

POLITICAL PERSPECTIVES ON THE IMPACT OF TOURISM ON SANTA FE

In an effort to explore how the issue of tourism's impact on Santa Fe was perceived from a political point of view, the current mayor of Santa Fe, Larry Delgado, and his two predecessors, Debbie Jaramillo and Sam Pick, were interviewed on their perspectives concerning the impact of tourism on the local population and their insights regarding Santa Fe's quality of life for local citizens. These three individuals have between them held the mayor's seat for most of the last quarter century.

Former Mayor Sam Pick

Former Santa Fe Mayor Sam Pick was in office for a total of ten years from 1978 to 1980 and from 1986 to 1994. Pick was mayor during what are considered the boom years in which tourism and development greatly expanded in the city. In an interview I conducted with the former mayor, Pick (2000) stated that Santa Fe needed to protect its uniqueness because its basic industry was still tourism. He commented, "Some locals may resent tourism but realistically it is Santa Fe's bread and butter. Tourism is a vital part of the Santa Fe economy. It keeps our sewers, libraries, and city services going. The taxes generated are important income to Santa Fe."

Rather than curbing tourism, Pick felt the city should improve its convention center and appeal to more affluent tourists who would spend more money while visiting the city. At the same time, Pick admitted that one problem that resulted from tourism was that tourists who later decided to become permanent residents of Santa Fe tended to drive up the cost of living for locals because, as Pick stated, "They will pay whatever is asked."

Pick said that the most important issues facing Santa Fe today are expanding employment opportunities in the city and improving the educational system. Pick believed that jobs need to be developed outside of the tourism industry, but a lack of quality public education in the city had led to a labor force that was not qualified to attract industry. He commented, "Many young people don't bother to get a high school diploma because they figure there are no jobs anyway. This is one reason for the high dropout rate. You don't need an education to work at McDonalds."

Pick characterized the Hispanic residents of Santa Fe as family-oriented people who had a strong sense of community, but he added that with a lack of job opportunities it was difficult for their children to stay in the city.

Former Mayor Debbie Jaramillo

Former Mayor Debbie Jaramillo was also interviewed for her perspective on the city and Hispanic cultural self-identity. Jaramillo (2000) believed that the same problems that existed for Hispanos in the past still are present today. She stated, "Unfortunately, I think the Hispanos in Santa Fe are in the same boat in the year 2000 that they've been in for centuries." She added, "How far up the ladder can you go making beds and cleaning toilets and washing dishes?"

Jaramillo saw Santa Fe as following the course that she had tried to change while she was in office. She said:

I see us promoting Santa Fe today just like we did before I came in. It's just like everything I did in those four years was just a big waste of time, you know. My whole motto was build from within, not from the outside. I kept talking homegrown, grow from within, take care of our own people. I'd point out the disparities you know, like housing. Where are we? We're on the southwest edges of town and all the homes we used to have belong to those from the outside. Where are we economically? We're on the lower end of the scale.

Jaramillo voiced a similar concern to one raised by Sam Pick regarding the educational system of Santa Fe. She explained, "Our kids in the public schools are numbers that are being pushed through the system to get Federal money, that's all they are. It's not really about making sure they know where they're going when they graduate. What's happening in the schools just extends to the rest of the community."

Debbie Jaramillo directed much of the blame for the decline of Hispanic influence in the city to Hispanic people themselves. She stated, "I don't see us going into the Millennium as an organized group, but just as a big number. We are the fastest-growing minority as we go into this Century but if we don't use it, we're just another number. I remember when I was running for office; I used to get more support calls from organizations in California, in Texas, Colorado. They were all calling me to see what they could do because they had heard about me, but I didn't get anything locally. It told me a lot about the Latino support and organization that was here. It would be nice if we could pull together but I just don't see it."

Jaramillo commented that many Santa Fe Hispanos still approach her and ask her to run for public office. She stated that they say to her, "We really need your voice, we need someone to speak for our people and I can't help but think, where were you when I was doing it? If we have that attitude, let someone else do it for us, it's never gonna get done."

Jaramillo added, "I'm afraid we may always be second-class citizens here, you know, it's like we've accepted that. Many local people, they've accepted that that's just the way it is."

Jaramillo summarized her efforts in changing the climate of Santa Fe in the following way: "I always saw myself as a change agent. I was someone who was going to stand up and not be afraid and show that it was okay to speak up, in hopes that others would follow."

Mayor Larry Delgado

Larry Delgado, the current mayor of Santa Fe, was elected in 1998, defeating Sam Pick and Debbie Jaramillo in the general election. Delgado was reelected for a second term in 2002 defeating reform candidate Patty Bushee who came in second, and Ike Pino, Debbie Jaramillo's brother, who placed third despite the fact that he outspent everyone and had the endorsement of former Mayor Sam Pick. I interviewed Mayor Delgado in his office at City Hall in order to obtain his impressions of the changes he had observed in Santa Fe and how these changes have affected the native Hispano population.

Delgado (2000) commented that he had seen a great deal of change in the city. He stated, "I saw Santa Fe, growing up here, when it was 20,000 and today, we're nearing 70,000 people in the city of Santa Fe and it has changed. It's growing and changing, the demographics are changing. I'm interested in seeing the new [2000] Census when it is completed to see how it has changed. When they did the last Census in 1990, we saw tremendous change. People are coming to live here. Our people that have been part of this community for generations; they are feeling these pressures."

Delgado was concerned about Santa Fe's economy being too dependent on tourism as its main industry. He explained, "I feel very uncomfortable about tourism being where we hang our hat, economically. Tourism and tourist-related facilities throughout the city probably bring us about 40 percent of our gross receipts, which we're dependent on. It becomes our general fund. It's how we fix streets and how we build parks and those kinds of things, but it's a roller coaster ride. One time we get a great tourist season, we do very well and then 'boom' we have a couple of years that we're down."

Delgado emphasized that he believed Santa Fe needed a more "integrated" economy in which tourism was not as dominant as a source of income. However, he said that in order for economic change to occur, native Santa Feans needed to focus on education in the community in order to create a skilled labor force. He stated:

> I would love not to have to say that 40 percent of our gross receipts come from tourism but it's an uphill battle. If you're a CEO and you come to me, you want to be able to know if the work force here

will be able to fill the jobs that you have. That's why we have to pound away that our people have to be educated.

Delgado believed that the common characterization of him as a central figure between Sam Pick's pro-tourism attitude and Debbie Jaramillo's reservations concerning tourism was fairly accurate. Delgado commented, "I think it's fair to characterize me as straddling the middle ground between Pick and Jaramillo. Tourism is important to us, it generates a lot of money and we need it. Now, give me something else that I can offset this with so I don't have to depend so much on it, but I can't just say, 'We don't want tourism.' I can't do that because I have responsibilities to make sure the city runs well, that I can meet payrolls."

Delgado voiced a pragmatic approach to the issue of growth in the city. He stated, "Santa Fe has changed. Sometimes changes happen for the better, sometimes they don't. As Mayor or City Councilors, we can't say 'We're going to shut down this town.' What's not living dies, but we can hope it's quality growth because it's going to happen. We're growing at about two-and-one-half percent a year."

Delgado believed that retaining Santa Fe Hispanic cultural identity in the face of the changes occurring in the city depended on educating the youth about their history and their culture. He cited groups like the Santa Fe Caballeros, the Fiesta Council, and Los Coloniales as examples of organizations providing such education. He also believed that public schools in Santa Fe needed to emphasize Hispanic cultural contributions in their curriculum to a greater degree.

Delgado stated that Santa Fe Hispanics needed to be "more aggressive, put ourselves out more." He commented, "It's a real interesting thing for me to look at a list of the members of the Chamber of Commerce. It tells you a lot. There are a few Hispanic names scattered in there, but it doesn't even come close to the demographics."

CONCLUSIONS

The question of how tourism has influenced Santa Fe Hispanic self-identity is evident in several ways. Santa Fe has derived considerable economic benefit from tourism during the twentieth century. However, a price has been paid for this prosperity. Many Santa Fe Hispanics have felt a sense of frustration as uncontrolled growth and unbridled tourism have changed the character of their city. Rising housing costs and gentrification have made it almost impossible for Santa Fe Hispanics, whose ancestors have lived in Santa Fe for generations, to purchase a home or pay escalating property taxes for homes they already own. Santa Fe Hispanics speak of feeling like second-class citizens in their ancestral city.

Santa Fe Hispanics also bemoan the loss of a sense of community in their city. The Santa Fe Plaza is often cited as a touchstone for what is happening to Santa Fe as a whole. High priced shops catering to tourists have replaced local businesses serving local citizens on the plaza. Although the three present and past mayors of Santa Fe had somewhat different interpretations of the challenges facing the Hispanic citizens in the city, several major points were consistently mentioned. First, the mayors addressed the fact that the tourism-based economy needs to be diversified in order to provide a stronger job base and to lessen dependence on just one source of revenue. Also, the educational system in the city needs to improve in order to provide local citizens with the skills needed to secure better jobs and to help the city attract new business.

Positive Hispanic cultural self-identity is closely tied to economic prosperity, along with a sense of control and self-worth that can only come with better economic opportunities for the Hispanic population of Santa Fe.

CHAPTER SEVEN

Conclusions

The exploration of Santa Fe Hispanic cultural self-identity in this text began with research into the historical factors that contributed to the formation of cultural identity. A major influence on Santa Fe Hispanic cultural self-identity that has been present from the earliest settlements to the present has been the role of Catholicism. Religious beliefs influenced Santa Fe Hispanic cultural life in almost all aspects during the settlement of Santa Fe and northern New Mexico. The role of the Catholic Church and the Penitente movement were vital in providing a sense of cultural self-identity for the colonists.

The remoteness of Santa Fe as a northern frontier separated by a long distance from the capital in Mexico City led to a geographical isolation that fostered the development of a unique culture in Santa Fe. Santa Fe's cultural flavor was influenced by Spain and Mexico in many aspects, but Santa Fe was distinct from either. These cultural differences are most clearly seen in the art, religion, and social practices of Hispanics in Santa Fe.

Intermarriage between the Spanish settlers and Pueblo Indians created a society in Santa Fe in which many of the inhabitants were descendants of racial mixing (Mestizos) and until the Mexican Revolution in 1821, an elaborate system of ethnic hierarchy (the casta system) was used to identify ethnicity and cultural position. Many Santa Feans who identify themselves as Hispanic today are descendants of Mestizo ancestors. In fact, it is probably difficult to find many Santa Fe Hispanics with long-term historical family ties to the city that do not possess a combination of Spanish and Indian blood. Acknowledgment of this racial mixing is often indicated by whether a Hispanic Santa Fean prefers the label "Spanish-American," "Hispanic," "Latino," or "Chicano."

Interest in tracing family bloodline is still great for some Santa Fe Hispanos. Fray Angélico Chávez's book *Origins of New Mexico Families in the Spanish Colonial Period*, published in 1954, continues to be an important source of information regarding records of original Spanish families who settled the region following the Oñate and De Vargas colonizations.

In his book, Chávez listed the names of many Spaniards who settled in Santa Fe and New Mexico and he provided information about their background and descendents. This study has allowed many Santa Fe Hispanics to research their own family names and point with pride to their Castilian roots.

American society has also had a profound effect on Santa Fe Hispanic culture. This influence began in 1821, with the Mexican government that came into power after the Mexican Revolution. The Mexican government permitted trade along the Santa Fe Trail and thus exposed Santa Fe to American influences.

The war between the United States and Mexico and the subsequent occupation of New Mexico by American military forces in 1846 dramatically changed the cultural climate of New Mexico. The U.S. doctrine of "Manifest Destiny" and the negative connotations of the Hispanic race stirred by the Mexican War put the Hispanic inhabitants of Santa Fe and New Mexico in the unaccustomed position of being the underclass race in a changing society. This trend continued through the late 1800s as Santa Fe fell more and more under the influence of American cultural sensibilities. Architecture changed to reflect the new power structure. The railroad brought in Anglo immigrants by the thousands. Eventually, Hispanic landowners were largely dispossessed, as 80 percent of their lands were reclaimed by lawyers, politicians, and land speculators.

The 1900s witnessed a renewed appreciation for Santa Fe's Hispanic culture, and adobe architecture. Disdained earlier, it was now admired. Santa Fe Hispanic cultural identity was profoundly affected by New Mexico's U.S. statehood. American ideals and national events such as World War I and World War II had far-reaching influences on cultural identity. Santa Fe became one of the prime tourist destinations in the United States, and Santa Fe Hispanics faced new challenges to their way of life as the tourist industry, expanded development, and a rising cost of living threatened their cultural landscape.

The information generated from interviews with Hispanic and non-Hispanic Santa Feans regarding their opinions about the major characteristics of Santa Fe Hispanic culture was similar for both groups of respondents. Hispanic and non-Hispanic Santa Fe residents cited religion, family, and food as the dominant characteristics that came to mind for them when they attempted to define Santa Fe Hispanic culture. The arts, Spanish language, and the Fiesta were also commonly cited.

There were not large differences of perceptions between Hispanic and non-Hispanic Santa Feans regarding the characteristics that they believed defined local Hispanic culture. There were concerns voiced that the local Hispanic culture needed to be protected and nurtured in order to be preserved, and that it was in danger of being diminished or lost if steps were not taken to maintain it.

In personal interviews with Santa Fe cultural leaders, educators, and historians, several themes emerged with regard to Santa Fe Hispanic culture. Several interviewees commented that the Santa Fe Hispanic culture was continually in a state of transformation but that change was not something to be feared. Historian Orlando Romero (2000) stated that the culture was "very much alive, but in transition." Tom Chávez (2000), director of the National Hispanic Cultural Center, emphasized that "strong cultures embrace outside influences" and he commented, "My fear is that we don't try to freeze the culture in a place and time because that will kill it." Rudolfo Anaya, acclaimed New Mexican author, and Father Jerome Martinez y Alire mirrored these sentiments in their interviews with *Crosswinds Weekly* (Garcia, 1999, July 22–29). Anaya stated that cultures were "organic and constantly changing." Martinez y Alire said, "Native Hispanic culture has always been evolving." Roberto Mondragon, a Santa Fe political and educational leader, and Ana Pacheco, publisher of *La Herencia*, both emphasized the importance of the Spanish language for maintaining Santa Fe Hispanic culture. Pacheco (2000) called the Spanish language "the glue that keeps the culture together." Romero and Mondragon emphasized the importance of Catholicism in Santa Fe Hispanic cultural self-identity. Chávez and Romero both commented on the unique character of Santa Fe because of its isolation from Spain and Mexico during the early years of its founding in the 1600s and 1700s.

Information gathered in these personal interviews with Santa Fe residents and leaders give a snapshot of the characteristics of Santa Fe

Hispanic culture. As cited earlier, the parameters of the concept of culture are so wide that it is almost impossible to define any culture adequately. As Orlando Romero (2000) commented, "Santa Fe Hispanic culture is not easily defined." Just as Santa Fe Hispanos differ in the labels they prefer (Hispanic, Latino, etc.), they have a variety of perspectives with regard to what defines their culture.

The Fiesta de Santa Fe as the major Hispanic cultural festival in Santa Fe is in many ways a barometer of local Hispanic cultural identity. As Elizabeth Rosa Lovato (1999), 1999 Fiesta queen, stated, "Fiesta is not a celebration of conquest to me; it's a celebration of culture." The Fiesta serves as a means of reinforcing and communicating Santa Fe Hispanic self-identity. It is a touchstone for many Santa Fe Hispanos who define the celebration as a source of cultural pride and unity and prefer not to emphasize any of the negative connotations associated with the reconquest of Santa Fe in 1692–1693.

Lustig and Koster (1999) stated that cultural identity is "one's sense of belonging to a particular culture or ethnic group," transmitted via "traditions, heritage, language, religion, ancestry, aesthetics, thinking patterns, and social structures" (p. 138). The Santa Fe Fiesta is a vehicle for each of these components within the context of the festival. As the 1999 Don Diego de Vargas of the Fiesta, Tommy Trujillo (1999), stated, "Taking classes for ten years wouldn't give me as much knowledge of my culture."

The Fiesta reflects many of the most important aspects of Santa Fe Hispanic culture. Religious faith in the form of the Fiesta masses and the prominence of La Conquistadora are central to the celebration. Language, ancestry and heritage, the arts, food, and connection to "place" are all celebrated during the Santa Fe Fiesta. Even though the Fiesta is touted as a community event for Santa Feans of all backgrounds, many aspects are strongly influenced by the local Hispanic culture.

Ironically, even the Santa Fe Fiesta, the main Hispanic cultural celebration in the city, is heavily influenced by the Anglo culture in a variety of ways. The Santa Fe Fiesta is both a self-defined and other-defined cultural festival for Santa Fe Hispanics. The merging of the Santa Fe Fiesta and Fourth of July celebrations in 1883 for the Tertio-Millennial Exposition was the beginning of Anglo influence on the Fiesta. This influence increased in 1919 when the Museum of New Mexico and its mainly Anglo staff revived the flagging Fiesta. Over the years, Anglo contributions to the Santa Fe Fiesta have included the Historical/Hysterical Parade, the introduction of a Fiesta queen and De Vargas role, the Children's Pet Parade, and of course Zozobra, who is sacrificed each Fiesta.

Another aspect of the Santa Fe Fiesta that Santa Fe Hispanics must grapple with is the historical legacy that the Fiesta carries. The celebration of the reconquest of Santa Fe has a number of inherent contradictions. Foremost is the idea of the "bloodless" reconquest of Santa Fe by the Spanish twelve years after the Pueblo Revolt in 1680. The historical facts indicate that the true reconquest occurred not in 1692, when the ritualized visit by De Vargas to Santa Fe occurred, but rather in 1693, when De Vargas returned with Spanish settlers to reclaim the property that the Pueblo Indians occupied. Some historians consider the less-idealized second visit of the Spaniards in 1693 to be the more legitimate reconquest of Santa Fe. This debate continues to linger in spite of many attempts by Fiesta organizers to downplay the second, more violent reconquest.

Art has played a vital role in the Santa Fe Hispanic community throughout the city's history. The early Spanish settlers used art as an important link to their cultural and religious roots as they built a life in the remote northern outpost of the Spanish Empire. New Mexico Spanish Colonial art developed in an environment with few physical resources and little formal artistic training. This aesthetic isolation from Spain, and later from Mexico, allowed Santa Fe and New Mexico folk art to develop its own unique style, influenced by, but in many ways different from, the art of the parent countries.

Spanish Colonial art in the region was almost exclusively religious in nature, reflecting the value that religion played in the colonists' lives. Additionally, Spanish Colonial art was valuable as a teaching tool in the effort to Christianize the Pueblo Indians. The language barrier between the Spaniards and the Pueblo people required the use of symbols and images to communicate religious concepts.

The latter half of the 1800s and the early part of the 1900s brought change to the Santa Fe art scene as Archbishop Lamy and the Catholic Church, and U.S. Anglo artists, brought their own aesthetic sensibilities and influences. With the coming of the railroad to Santa Fe in the late 1800s,

American aesthetics strongly impacted the indigenous Hispanic culture.

The once-dominant Hispanic aesthetic position in the city was now regulated to the lowest status, behind Anglo "fine art" and Pueblo Indian art, which was viewed in the "noble-savage" context. The cultural denigration of the Hispano population, an extension of the "Hispanophobia" perpetuated during the Mexican War, was reflected in the attitudes toward Hispano art that was categorized as only being "folk art" and not capable of reaching "fine art" status. In many ways, this attitude toward Santa Fe Hispanic art persists to the present day. Many of the comments collected in my interviews indicated that Santa Fe Hispano artists still feel the sting of this mind-set. A major question voiced by several local Hispano artists who were interviewed was: How do Santa Fe Hispano artists retain and honor traditions in art without it becoming a limitation that does not allow development beyond the past? Many current Hispano artists desire to expand beyond the folk-art label and not allow ethnicity to overshadow their art.

The need for empowerment[1] was a concern raised by many artists interviewed. This desire for a more expansive cultural self-identity reflected in the arts was often voiced.

Kirk (1994) wrote that an authentic place could be used as a source of identity. The struggle that confronts many Hispanic Santa Feans is how to maintain authenticity in a city that has become a major tourist destination. A key question is whether Santa Fe is becoming "inauthentic" in order to serve the tourism industry. Many Santa Fe Hispanics feel the cultural changes taking place are not within their control. They fear the city is being exploited, commercialized, and developed without regard to long-term consequences for them. Kirk (1994) stated, "If a place becomes placeless through reduction or erosion of its symbols by mass culture, the people who used this place for a source of identity could lose that source" (p. 82).

This statement summarizes the misgivings that many Hispanic Santa Feans feel when they reflect on the changes taking place in their city. The strongest voice for this concern was the former mayor of Santa Fe, Debbie Jaramillo, whose 1994 election was a reflection of these reservations.

In addition to concern over the commercialization of their culture, many Santa Fe Hispanics struggle with economic issues related to rampant tourism and development. The skyrocketing costs of housing and property taxes are difficult to contend with, particularly given the fact that many of the jobs associated with the tourism industry tend to be low-paying, service-related positions. Santa Fe Hispanics whose lives and culture have been dramatically altered by tourism and development tend to feel a sense of powerlessness over the changes that have occurred. If the gentrification of Santa Fe is not abated, Debbie Jaramillo's now renowned quote, "They painted the downtown brown and moved the brown people out," may yet come to pass.

Defining cultural self-identity for a particular population is a complex undertaking involving a multitude of factors. If culture is, as Rogers and Steinfatt (1999) described it, "The total way of life of a people, composed of the learned and shared behavior patterns, values, norms and material objects" (p. 14), then a complete understanding of culture and the cultural identity of any group is a task almost infinite in nature. This book can aspire to explore only a selected number of aspects in relation to the cultural self-identity of the Santa Fe Hispanic population.

Santa Fe Hispanic cultural self-identity is unavoidably influenced by the fact that Santa Fe is a tourist town in which local culture and local history have been made into commodities for sale by the tourism industry. The issue of cultural identity formation transmitted by members of an individual's own cultural group (self-defined identity) or by people and cultures outside of the individual's cultural group (other-defined identity) is of particular importance in this environment.

The question of how each identity has affected the other is a complex issue. The push since the early 1900s to promote Santa Fe as a tourist haven has redefined Hispanic culture from the early Anglo-American perception of it as inferior and backward to a new definition of Santa Fe Hispanic culture as exotic and romantic. The Hispanic people of Santa Fe have simultaneously rejected and internalized these other-defined stereo-types to differing degrees during the past century. The state museum system has generally provided a more balanced picture of Hispanic history and identity than commercial interests, allowing those with the interest and motivation to explore Hispano culture in a more realistic fashion.

The challenge of trying to maintain and understand cultural self-iden-tity in a tourist mecca is not unique to Santa Fe. This struggle occurs with native Hawaiians, Chinese San Franciscans, and other ethnic groups worldwide. The struggle between self-defined and other-defined cultural identity is intensified as old traditions and customs fall away in an ever-more homogenized world that espouses mass cultural views that infiltrate native cultures, making their members susceptible to accepting simplified stereotypes of themselves and their own culture. These cultural pressures often cause anger and resentment for some within the culture as they try to hold on to the last vestiges of their own authentic cultural identity apart from commerce and tourism concerns. These concerned natives protest that their culture does not exist simply for the benefit and enjoyment of others. For example, Santa Fe Hispanics have often voiced resentment about the transformation of the Santa Fe Plaza from a community meeting place to a tourist-shopping venue. They wonder if Santa Fe exists primarily for its native inhabitants or as a playground for outsiders.

A key question is: At what point do the stereotypes and myths surrounding a culture become the reality? All cultures to a certain extent can be said to be in many ways "mythical creations." What may be important is not so much that cultures contain myth but rather who "controls" the development and the perpetuation of these myths. Is it the "inside" group or the "other" that holds the influence? This issue is one of power and self-determination. The question may be asked: Who creates the social constructionism that defines the culture in question? When looking at the issue of authenticity versus invented traditions, people often create reality and invent language to reinforce their perspective.

Santa Fe's cultural landscape has gone through many perceptual shifts during its history. An example was the view following the U.S. occupation in 1846 that Santa Fe's adobe architecture was backward and undesirable. This perception began to change in the 1900s, and today adobe construction in the city is considered the most prestigious. "Santa Fe style" furnishings, art, clothing, and various other goods are all artifacts of an invented cultural tradition. Even the historical revisionism of the "bloodless" reconquest of Santa Fe that is celebrated during the annual Santa Fe Fiesta is an example of liberal shifts in social constructionism that have taken place in the city throughout its history.

No wonder that confusion exists in regard to cultural self-identity for

Santa Fe Hispanics who live in a city in which the definition of their culture is continually shifting and transforming.

The study of culture and the formation of cultural identity are being conducted by scholars from various disciplines internationally. Each contribution adds another piece to the larger puzzle of understanding the human family. As more scholars study their indigenous cultures in the future, the academic community will be enriched by new voices providing an insider's perspective to the existing literature.

Notes

CHAPTER 1

1. *Social constructionism* is defined as "the perception of an individual, group, or idea that is constructed through cultural and social practice, but appears to be 'natural' or the way things are" (*Equal Employment and Civil Rights Journal*, 1999, p. 5).

2. *Commodification* is defined as the process of placing a market or monetary value on something. In the present study, the term is used in relation to the attempt to make the culture of Santa Fe into a revenue-generating product.

CHAPTER 3

1. The importance of language in defining and preserving culture has been cited by numerous scholars. The Sapir-Whorf hypothesis, an intercultural communication theory, contends that language profoundly affects the nature of people's thoughts and thus their perception of the world and subsequently their behavior.

2. "MEChA" stands for the *Movimieto Estudiantil Chicano de Aztlán*. Created in 1969 at the University of California, Santa Barbara, MEChA was a coalition of many student groups that existed since the early 1960s. MEChA was an important part of the Chicano civil rights movement and is still active nationally in many schools and universities.

3. *Values* are defined as fundamental, deep-seated truths or themes about what is correct or good and bad according to one's personal or a group's doctrine. *Beliefs* are defined as an understanding by an individual or group about the outside world and what is true and false.

CHAPTER 4

1. Santa Fe Hispanic native Francisco "Pancho" Ortega was shot on Hickox Street in Santa Fe by the police after he had earlier threatened to kill himself with a steak knife. Police and some witnesses say he lunged with a knife at a group of eight officers who had surrounded him, but other witnesses have disputed that version of the events. For some people, the Ortega shooting symbolized the economic injustice and tensions between Hispanics and Anglos in Santa Fe, even though the majority of the Santa Fe police force was Hispanic (Terrell, 1993, September 10, pp. A1, A3).

2. The Santa Fe Fiesta Council is a nonprofit organization that oversees the annual Santa Fe Fiesta. All members of the Fiesta Council are volunteers. Membership is open to any interested citizen, but a Santa Fe Fiesta Council membership committee must screen members before they are accepted. Membership has historically been and continues to be primarily Hispanic.

CHAPTER 6

1. Kirk (1994) defined *authenticity* as "the possession of verifiable (by some set of standards) qualities of genuineness or realness (e.g., an authentic work of art), and also to that which is true, moral, and connected (e.g., an authentic self)" (pp. 1–2).

CHAPTER 7

1. *Empowerment* is defined by Rogers and Steinfatt (1999) as "the degree to which an individual perceives that she or he controls her/his situation" (pp. 249–50).

References

Adams, Eleanor B., and Fray Angélico Chávez. 1956. *The Missions of New Mexico, 1776: A Description by Fray Francisco Atanasio Dominguez with Other Contemporary Documents.* Albuquerque: University of New Mexico Press.

Bright, Brenda Jo, and Liza Bakewell, eds. 1995. *Looking High and Low: Art and Cultural Identity.* Tucson: University of Arizona Press.

Bustamante, Adrian H. 1989. "Españoles, Castas, y Labradores: Santa Fe Society in the Eighteenth Century." In D. G. Noble, ed., *Santa Fe: History of an Ancient City*, pp. 65–77. Santa Fe, NM: School of American Research Press.

Campa, Arthur L. 1979. *Hispanic Culture in the Southwest.* Norman: University of Oklahoma Press.

Carrillo, Charles. 2000. Personal Interview with Charles M. Carrillo (Santa Fe *santero*) on March 24, 2000, by Andrew Lovato (in Santa Fe, NM).

Chávez, Fray Angélico. 1954. *Origins of New Mexico Families in the Spanish Colonial Period.* Santa Fe: The Historical Society of New Mexico.

Chávez, Thomas E. 1985. "Santa Fe's Own: A History of Fiesta." In D. Pierce, D., ed., *Vivan las Fiestas*, pp. 6–17. Santa Fe: Museum of New Mexico Press.

———. 2000. Personal Interview with Thomas E. Chávez (Director, Palace of the Governors) on January 20, 2000, by Andrew Lovato (Santa Fe, NM).

Chicano/LatinoNet.com (2002). http://www.azteca.net/chicano.html. University of Southern California.

City of Santa Fe Convention and Visitors Bureau. 1999. *The Official 1999 Santa Fe Visitors Guide.* Santa Fe, NM: Starlight Publishing.

———. 2004. *The Official 2004 Santa Fe Visitors Guide.* Santa Fe, NM: Starlight Media Group.

City of Santa Fe Planning and Land Use Department. 2000. Santa Fe Trends 2003. Santa Fe, NM.

———. 2003. Santa Fe Trends 2000. Santa Fe, NM.

Coan, Charles F. 1925. *A History of New Mexico.* Chicago: The American Historical Society.

Cohen, Erik. 1988. Authenticity and Commoditization in Tourism. *Annals of Tourism Research* 15: 371–86.

Davila, Erika. 1999, Artists Petition for Space at Spanish Market. *The Santa Fe New Mexican*, July 25. pp. B1, B5.

———. 1999, ¿Que viva las Fiestas? *The Santa Fe New Mexican*, September 7. pp. A1–A2.

———. 1999, A Low-key Burn. *The Santa Fe New Mexican*, September 10. pp. A1–A2.

De Kadt, Emanuel. 1979. *Tourism: Passport to Development? Perspectives on the Social and Cultural Effects of Tourism on Developing Countries.* New York: Oxford University Press.

Dean, Rob, ed. 1999, The 287th Fiesta De Santa Fe Official Program. *The Santa Fe New Mexican*, September 4. pp. 3–19.

Delgado, Larry. 2000. Personal Interview with Larry Delgado (Santa Fe mayor) on May 25, 2000, by Andrew Lovato (Santa Fe, NM).

The diversity dictionary. 1999. *Equal Employment and Civil Rights Journal* 4 (4).

Duke, Biddle. 1992, Along with Fiesta, Priest Has Changed with Time. *The Santa Fe New Mexican*, September 7. pp. A1, A3.

Easthouse, Keith. 1993, Leaders Call Fiesta Offensive. *The Santa Fe New Mexican*, September 12. pp. A1, A3.

Eldredge, Charles C., ed. 1986. *Art in New Mexico, 1900–1945: Paths to Taos and Santa Fe*. New York: Abbeville Press.

Ellis, Simone. 1993. *Santa Fe Art*. Avenel, NJ: Crescent Books.

Fuentes, Carlos. 1992. *The Buried Mirror: Reflections on Spain and the New World*. New York: Houghton Mifflin.

Gablik, Suzi. 1995. *Conversations before the End of Time*. New York: Thames and Hudson.

Garcia, David A. 1999, Nuestra Rica Hispanidad: Is the Culture Fading? *Crosswinds Weekly*, July 22–29. pp. 8–11.

Graburn, Nelson H. H. 1983. The Anthropology of Tourism. *Annals of Tourism Research* 10 (3): 9–33.

———.1976. *Ethnic and Tourist Arts: Cultural Expressions from the Fourth World*. Berkeley: University of California Press.

Grimes, Ronald. 1976. *Symbol and conquest: Public ritual and drama in Santa Fe*. Ithaca, NY: Cornell University Press.

Griswold Del Castillo, Richard, Teresa McKenna, and Yvonne Yarbo-Bejarno, eds. 1991. *Chicano Art: Resistance and Affirmation. 1965–1985*. Los Angeles: University of California.

Grunstein, Miguel, producer. 1995. *La villa de Santa Fe* [videotape]. Albuquerque: KNME-TV and University of New Mexico.

Guzmán, Gilberto. 2000. Personal Interview with Gilberto Guzmán (Santa Fe artist) on April 4, 2000, by Andrew Lovato (in Santa Fe, NM).

Gutiérrez, Ramon A. 1991. *When Jesus Came the Corn Mothers Went Away: Marriage, Sexuality, and Power in New Mexico, 1500–1846*. Stanford, CA: Stanford University Press.

Hall, Edward T. 1959. *The Silent Language*. New York: Anchor Books.

———. 1976. *Beyond Culture*. New York: Doubleday.

———. 1986. Foreword. In J. Collier and M. Collier, *Visual Anthropology: Photography as a Research Method*, p. xvii. Albuquerque: University of New Mexico Press.

———. 1999. Personal Interview with Edward T. Hall (intercultural communication author and scholar) on October 25, 1999, by Andrew Lovato (in Santa Fe, NM).

Hammond, George P., and Thomas C. Donnelly. 1936. *The Story of New Mexico: Its History and Government*. Albuquerque: University of New Mexico Press.

Jaramillo, Debbie. 2000. Personal Interview with Debbie Jaramillo (former Santa Fe mayor) on May 10, 2000, by Andrew Lovato (in Santa Fe, NM).

Jules-Rosette, Bennetta. 1984. *The Messages of Tourist Art: An African Semiotic System in Comparative Perspective*. New York: Plenum Press.

Kessell, John L. 1979. *Kiva, Cross and Crown: The Pecos Indians and New Mexico 1540–1840*. Washington D.C.: National Park Service, U.S. Department of the Interior.

———. 1989. By Force of Arms: Vargas and the Spanish Restoration of Santa Fe. In D. G. Noble, ed., *Santa Fe: History of an Ancient City*, pp. 53–63. Santa Fe, NM: School of American Research Press.

Kirk, Camille M. 1994. Authenticity and Place: An Interpretation of Resident Response to Tourism in Santa Fe, New Mexico. Master's thesis, University of California, Los Angeles.

Kusel, Denise, and Craig Smith, eds. 1999, 150 Years: 1849–1999. *The Santa Fe New Mexican*, July. pp. 36–45.

LeCompte, Janet. 1989. When Santa Fe Was a Mexican Town: 1821 to 1846. In D. G. Noble, ed., *Santa Fe: History of an Ancient City*, pp. 79–95. Santa Fe, NM: School of American Research Press.

Leyba, Sam. 2000. Personal Interview with Sam Leyba (Santa Fe artist and activist) on April 4, 2000, by Andrew Lovato (in Santa Fe, NM).

Lippard, Lucy R. 1999. *On the Beaten Path*. New York: New Press.

López, Antonio. 1998, El Museo Cultural: A Dream Becomes a Reality. *The Santa Fe New Mexican*, May 15. Pasatiempo, p. 29.

———. 1999. Xeroxing Culture, Erasing History. *Arté* 1 (1): 17–24.

López, Ramón José. 2002. Personal Interview with Ramón José López (Santa Fe artist) on May 15, 2002, by Andrew Lovato (in Santa Fe, NM).

Lovato, Elizabeth R. 1999. Personal Interview with Elizabeth Rosa Lovato (1999 Fiesta queen) on December 3, 1999, by Andrew Lovato (in Santa Fe, NM).

Lustig, Myron W., and Jolene Koester. 1999. *Intercultural Communication: Interpersonal Communication across Cultures*. 3d ed. New York: Longman.

MacCannell, Dean. 1976. *The Tourist: A New Theory of the Leisure Class*. New York: Schocken Books.

Martinez, Roger. 1999. Personal Interview with Roger Martinez (Fiesta participant) on December 11, 1999, by Andrew Lovato (in Santa Fe, NM).

Mather, Christine, ed. 1983. *Colonial Frontiers: Art and life in Spanish New Mexico, the Fred Harvey Collection*. Santa Fe, NM: International Folk Art Foundation.

Mathieson, Alister, and Geoffrey Wall. 1982. *Tourism: Economic, Physical and Social Impacts*. New York: Longman Scientific and Technical Press.

Messerli, Hannah R. 1995. Tourism Area Life Cycles and Residents' Perceptions: The Case of Santa Fe, New Mexico. Ph.D. diss., Cornell University. University Microfilms no. 9333202.

Mondragon, Roberto. 2000. Personal Interview with Roberto Mondragon (Santa Fe Aspectos Culturales) on January 4, 2000, by Andrew Lovato (in Santa Fe, NM).

Neary, Ben. 1997, The Mayor that Roars. *The Santa Fe New Mexican*, December 21. pp. A1, A6.

Novak, Shonda. 2000, A Question of Many Colors. *The Santa Fe New Mexican*, March 6. pp. A1, A3.

Novas, Himilce. 1994. *Everything You Need to Know about Latino History*. New York: Penguin Books.

Nunn, Tey Marianna. 1998. Creating for El Diablo a Pie: The Hispana and Hispano Artists of the Works Progress Administration in New Mexico. Ph.D. diss., University of New Mexico. University Microfilms no. 9839219.

————. 2000. Personal Interview with Tey Marianna Nunn (Santa Fe museum curator) on April 10, 2000, by Andrew Lovato (Santa Fe, NM).

Ozen, Hamiyet. 1994. A Model for the Study of the Impact of Growth of Tourism on Historic Sites in Santa Fe, New Mexico, and San Antonio, Texas. Ph.D. diss., Texas Tech University, 1994. University Microfilms no. 9426768.

Pacheco, Ana. 2000. Personal Interview with Ana Pacheco (publisher of *La Herencia*) on January 21, 2000, by Andrew Lovato (in Santa Fe, NM).

Padilla, Carmella. 1999. Making Hispanic History: The Spanish Colonial Arts Society Museum. *1999 Spanish Market Magazine*. Santa Fe, NM: Spanish Colonial Arts Society.

Perrigo, Lynn I. 1964. *The Rio Grande Adventure: A History of New Mexico*. Chicago: Lyons and Carnahan.

————. 1971. *The American Southwest: Its People and Cultures*. Albuquerque: University of New Mexico Press.

Pick, Sam. 2000. Personal Interview with Sam Pick (former Santa Fe mayor) on May 10, 2000, by Andrew Lovato (in Santa Fe, NM).

Porter, Richard E., and Larry A. Samovar. 1997. *Intercultural Communication: A Reader*. 8th ed. New York: Wadsworth.

Quick, Bob. 1999, Median Cost of a Home in Santa Fe Reaches All-time High—again. *The Santa Fe New Mexican*, October 8. pp. A1, A4.

Reyna, Diane, and Jeannette DeBouzek, producers. 1992. *Gathering Up Again: Fiesta in Santa Fe* [videotape]. Albuquerque, NM: Quotidian Independent Documentary Research.

Ribera-Ortega, Pedro. 1999. Personal Interview with Pedro Ribera-Ortega (Fiesta historian) on December 17, 1999, by Andrew Lovato (in Santa Fe, NM).

Robertson, Edna C. 1974. *Handbook of the Collections, 1917–1974: Museum of Fine Arts*. Santa Fe: Museum of New Mexico.

Rodriguez, Sylvia. 1989. Art, Tourism, and Race Relations in Taos: Toward a Sociology of the Art Colony. *Journal of Anthropological Research* 45 (1): 77–99.

Rodriguez, Sylvia, Christine Sierra, and Felipe Gonzales, producers. 1999. *This Town Is Not for Sale: The 1994 Santa Fe Mayoral Election* [videotape]. Albuquerque: KNME-TV and University of New Mexico.

Rogers, Everett M., and Thomas M. Steinfatt. 1999. *Intercultural Communication*. Prospect Heights, IL: Waveland Press.

Romero, Orlando. 1992, Doing Fiesta a Disservice. *The Santa Fe Reporter*, July 8–14. p. 10.

———. 2000. Personal Interview with Orlando Romero (Santa Fe writer and historian) on January 21, 2000, by Andrew Lovato (in Santa Fe, NM).

Rosenak, Chuck, and Jan Rosenak. 1998. *The Saint Makers: Contemporary Santeras y Santeros*. Flagstaff, AZ: Northland Publishing.

Samaniego, AnaMaria. 2000. Personal Interview with AnaMaria Samaniego (Santa Fe artist) on March 27, 2000, by Andrew Lovato (in Santa Fe, NM).

Santa Fe County Chamber of Commerce. 1999. *1999 Business Reference and Community Guide*. Santa Fe, NM: HK Advertising.

Santa Fe Market Profile. 1999, *New Mexico Business Weekly*, December 13–19. pp. 2, 7.

Selcraig, Bruce. 1994, Glitz and Growth Take a Major Hit in Santa Fe. *High Country News* 26 (14), (August 8): 1, 10–12.

Shalkop, Robert L. 1967. *Wooden Santos: The Santos of New Mexico*. Colorado Springs: Taylor Museum of the Colorado Springs Fine Arts Center.

Sherman, John. 1996. *Santa Fe: A pictorial history*. 2d ed. Virginia Beach, VA: Donning Company.

Shimmel, Julie. 1986. The Hispanic Southwest. In C. C. Eldredge, ed., *Art in New Mexico, 1900–1945: Paths to Taos and Santa Fe*, pp. 101–45. New York: Abbeville Press.

Simmons, Marc. 1988. *New Mexico: An Interpretive History*. Albuquerque: University of New Mexico Press.

———. 1991. *The Last Conquistador: Juan de Oñate and the Settling of the Far Southwest*. Norman: University of Oklahoma Press.

———. 1998. *New Mexico!* 2d ed. Albuquerque: University of New Mexico Press.

Sorrells, Kathryn. 1999. Women Creating New Mexico: Intercultural Communication Processes in Southwest Forms of Creative Expression. Ph.D. diss., University of New Mexico. University Microfilms no. 9939986.

Stieber, Tamar. 1998 Focus on Santa Fe. *New Mexico Business Journal*, (December): 27–39.

Terrell, Steve. 1993, Let Fiesta Be a 'Time of Reconciliation.' *The Santa Fe New Mexican*, September 10. pp. A1, A3.

Trujillo, Tommy. 1999. Personal Interview with Tommy Trujillo (1999 De Vargas) on December 17, 1999, by Andrew Lovato (in Santa Fe, NM).

Twitchell, Ralph E. 1911. *Leading Facts of New Mexico History*. Vol. 1. Cedar Rapids, Iowa: The Torch Press.

———. 1912. *Leading Facts of New Mexico History*. Vol. 2. Cedar Rapids, Iowa: The Torch Press.

Udall, Sharyn. 1987. *Santa Fe Art Colony, 1900–1942*. Santa Fe, NM: Gerald Peters Art Gallery.

Udall, Sharyn, and J. Connors. 1986. Artists' Biographies. In C. C. Eldredge, ed., *Art in New Mexico, 1900–1945: Paths to Taos and Santa Fe*, pp. 101–45. New York: Abbeville Press.

Urry, John. 1990. *The Tourist Gaze: Leisure and Travel in Contemporary Societies*. Newbury Park, CA: Sage.

Utgaard, Mark C. 1990, Museum Vows showings of Hispanic, Indian art. *The Santa Fe New Mexican*, May 6. p. D1.

Valdez, Valdez Abeyta y. 2000. Personal Interview with Valdez Abeyta y Valdez (Santa Fe museum administrator) on March 28, 2000, by Andrew Lovato (in Santa Fe, NM).

Vigil, Frederico. 1999. Personal Interview with Frederico Vigil (Santa Fe artist) on April 12, 1999, by Andrew Lovato (in Santa Fe, NM).

Villani, John. 1996, Museum a Vision of History. *The Albuquerque Journal*, January 21. pp. D1–D3.

Weigle, Marta. 1976. *Brothers of Light, Brothers of Blood: The Penitentes of the Southwest*. Albuquerque: University of New Mexico Press.

Wilson, Chris. 1997. *The Myth of Santa Fe*. Albuquerque: University of New Mexico Press.

Wilson, John P. 1989. The American Occupation of Santa Fe: "My Government Will Correct All This." In D. G. Noble, ed., *Santa Fe: History of an Ancient City*, pp. 97–113. Santa Fe, NM: School of American Research Press.

Witkin, Stanley L. 1999. Constructing Our Future. *Social Work* 44, (1): 5–8.

Index